Microsoft® Office Outlook® 2010

Level 1

Microsoft® Office Outlook® 2010: Level 1

Part Number: 084595
Course Edition: 1.0

NOTICES

DISCLAIMER: While Element K Corporation takes care to ensure the accuracy and quality of these materials, we cannot guarantee their accuracy, and all materials are provided without any warranty whatsoever, including, but not limited to, the implied warranties of merchantability or fitness for a particular purpose. The name used in the data files for this course is that of a fictitious company. Any resemblance to current or future companies is purely coincidental. We do not believe we have used anyone's name in creating this course, but if we have, please notify us and we will change the name in the next revision of the course. Element K is an independent provider of integrated training solutions for individuals, businesses, educational institutions, and government agencies. Use of screenshots, photographs of another entity's products, or another entity's product name or service in this book is for editorial purposes only. No such use should be construed to imply sponsorship or endorsement of the book by, nor any affiliation of such entity with Element K. This courseware may contain links to sites on the Internet that are owned and operated by third parties (the "External Sites"). Element K is not responsible for the availability of, or the content located on or through, any External Site. Please contact Element K if you have any concerns regarding such links or External Sites.

TRADEMARK NOTICES Element K and the Element K logo are trademarks of Element K Corporation and its affiliates.

Outlook is a registered trademark of Microsoft Corporation in the U.S. and other countries; the Microsoft products and services discussed or described may be trademarks of Microsoft Corporation. All other product names and services used throughout this course may be common law or registered trademarks of their respective proprietors.

Copyright © 2010 Element K Corporation. All rights reserved. Screenshots used for illustrative purposes are the property of the software proprietor. This publication, or any part thereof, may not be reproduced or transmitted in any form or by any means, electronic or mechanical, including photocopying, recording, storage in an information retrieval system, or otherwise, without express written permission of Element K, 500 Canal View Boulevard, Rochester, NY 14623, (585) 240-7500, (800) 478-7788. Element K Courseware's World Wide Web site is located at **www.elementkcourseware.com**.

This book conveys no rights in the software or other products about which it was written; all use or licensing of such software or other products is the responsibility of the user according to terms and conditions of the owner. Do not make illegal copies of books or software. If you believe that this book, related materials, or any other Element K materials are being reproduced or transmitted without permission, please call (800) 478-7788.

HELP US IMPROVE OUR COURSEWARE

Your comments are important to us. Please contact us at Element K Press LLC, 1-800-478-7788, 500 Canal View Boulevard, Rochester, NY 14623, Attention: Product Planning, or through our Web site at **http://support.elementkcourseware.com**.

Microsoft® Office Outlook® 2010: Level 1

Lesson 1: Getting Started with Outlook
    A. Identify the Components of the Outlook Interface 2
    B. Read an Email Message. 15
    C. Reply to and Forward an Email Message 23
    D. Print an Email Message 27
    E. Delete an Email Message. 30

Lesson 2: Composing Messages
    A. Create an Email Message 36
    B. Format a Message 41
    C. Check Spelling and Grammar 46
    D. Attach a File 53
    E. Enhance an Email Message 56
    F. Send an Email Message 70

Lesson 3: Organizing Messages
    A. Manage Email Messages. 76
    B. Move Email Messages into Folders 84
    C. Open and Save an Attachment 91

Lesson 4: Managing Contacts
    A. Add a Contact 98
    B. Sort and Find Contacts 112
    C. Find the Geographical Location of a Contact 116
    D. Update Contacts 118

Lesson 5: Scheduling Appointments

    A. Explore the Outlook Calendar.................................. **128**

    B. Schedule an Appointment..................................... **132**

    C. Edit Appointments... **140**

Lesson 6: Managing Meetings in Outlook

    A. Schedule a Meeting.. **146**

    B. Reply to a Meeting Request................................... **158**

    C. Track and Update Scheduled Meetings **162**

    D. Print the Calendar **168**

Lesson 7: Managing Tasks and Notes

    A. Create a Task **172**

    B. Edit and Update a Task **179**

    C. Create a Note **182**

    D. Edit a Note... **186**

Lesson Labs.. **191**

Solutions **199**

Glossary **201**

Index **203**

About This Course

This course is the first in a series of three Microsoft® Office Outlook® 2010 courses. It will provide you with the skills you need to start sending and responding to email in Microsoft® Office Outlook® 2010, as well as maintaining your Calendar. In this course, you will explore the user interface of Outlook, compose and send email, schedule appointments, manage contact information, organize meetings, and create tasks and notes in Outlook.

On any busy day, it is a challenge to keep up with your daily correspondence, appointments, meetings, and tasks. Having a tool capable of keeping large amounts of information organized and at your fingertips could mean the difference between falling behind and staying on track. Microsoft Office Outlook 2010 is one such tool that you can use to effectively communicate electronically and be organized.

Course Description

Target Student

This course is intended for people who have a basic understanding of Microsoft Windows and want to know how to use Outlook to manage their time and information.

Course Prerequisites

To be successful in this course, you should be familiar with using personal computers. You should be comfortable in the Windows environment and be able to use Windows to manage information. Specifically, you should be able to launch and close programs; navigate to information stored on a computer; and manage files and folders. To ensure your success, we recommend that you first take one of Element K's introductory Windows courses, such as either of the following, or have equivalent skills and knowledge:

- *Windows XP Professional: Level 1* or;
- *Windows XP: Introduction*

Course Objectives

In this course, you will use Outlook to compose and send email, schedule appointments and meetings, manage contact information, schedule tasks, and create notes.

You will:

- Explore the Outlook interface, send mail, and respond to messages.

- Compose email messages.
- Organize email messages into folders.
- Manage contacts and contact information.
- Schedule appointments.
- Schedule a meeting.
- Manage tasks and notes.

How to Use This Book

As a Learning Guide

This book is divided into lessons and topics, covering a subject or a set of related subjects. In most cases, lessons are arranged in order of increasing proficiency.

The results-oriented topics include relevant and supporting information you need to master the content. Each topic has various types of activities designed to enable you to practice the guidelines and procedures as well as to solidify your understanding of the informational material presented in the course.

At the back of the book, you will find a glossary of the definitions of the terms and concepts used throughout the course. You will also find an index to assist in locating information within the instructional components of the book.

In the Classroom

This book is intended to enhance and support the in-class experience. Procedures and guidelines are presented in a concise fashion along with activities and discussions. Information is provided for reference and reflection in such a way as to facilitate understanding and practice.

Each lesson may also include a Lesson Lab or various types of simulated activities. You will find the files for the simulated activities along with the other course files on the enclosed CD-ROM. If your course manual did not come with a CD-ROM, please go to **http://elementkcourseware.com** to download the files. If included, these interactive activities enable you to practice your skills in an immersive business environment, or to use hardware and software resources not available in the classroom. The course files that are available on the CD-ROM or by download may also contain sample files, support files, and additional reference materials for use both during and after the course.

As a Teaching Guide

Effective presentation of the information and skills contained in this book requires adequate preparation. As such, as an instructor, you should familiarize yourself with the content of the entire course, including its organization and approaches. You should review each of the student activities and exercises so you can facilitate them in the classroom.

Throughout the book, you may see Instructor Notes that provide suggestions, answers to problems, and supplemental information for you, the instructor. You may also see references to "Additional Instructor Notes" that contain expanded instructional information; these notes appear in a separate section at the back of the book. PowerPoint slides may be provided on the included course files, which are available on the enclosed CD-ROM or by download from **http://elementkcourseware.com.** The slides are also referred to in the text. If you plan to use the slides, it is recommended to display them during the corresponding content as indicated in the instructor notes in the margin.

The course files may also include assessments for the course, which can be administered diagnostically before the class, or as a review after the course is completed. These exam-type questions can be used to gauge the students' understanding and assimilation of course content.

As a Review Tool

Any method of instruction is only as effective as the time and effort you, the student, are willing to invest in it. In addition, some of the information that you learn in class may not be important to you immediately, but it may become important later. For this reason, we encourage you to spend some time reviewing the content of the course after your time in the classroom.

As a Reference

The organization and layout of this book make it an easy-to-use resource for future reference. Taking advantage of the glossary, index, and table of contents, you can use this book as a first source of definitions, background information, and summaries.

Course Icons

Icon	Description
	A **Caution Note** makes students aware of potential negative consequences of an action, setting, or decision that are not easily known.
	Display Slide provides a prompt to the instructor to display a specific slide. Display Slides are included in the Instructor Guide only.
	An **Instructor Note** is a comment to the instructor regarding delivery, classroom strategy, classroom tools, exceptions, and other special considerations. Instructor Notes are included in the Instructor Guide only.
	Notes Page indicates a page that has been left intentionally blank for students to write on.
	A **Student Note** provides additional information, guidance, or hints about a topic or task.
	A **Version Note** indicates information necessary for a specific version of software.

Course Requirements and Setup

You can find a list of hardware and software requirements to run this class as well as detailed classroom setup procedures in the course files that are available on the CD-ROM that shipped with this book. If your course manual did not come with a CD-ROM, please go to **http://www.elementk.com/courseware-file-downloads** to download the files.

1 Getting Started with Outlook

Lesson Time: 1 hour(s), 15 minutes

Lesson Objectives:

In this lesson, you will explore the Outlook interface, send mail, and respond to messages.

You will:

- Identify the components of the Outlook 2010 environment.
- Read an email message.
- Reply to an email message.
- Print an email message.
- Delete an email message.

Introduction

You may handle a large amount of business communication in your organization, which has a mail management application in place. You need to get familiar with the interface of the Outlook application to read and respond to messages, print a copy of a message, and delete messages. In this lesson, you will start using Outlook.

Before using Outlook, you may want to get familiar with its interface and know how to use it to read messages and respond to them. Being able to identify the interface components and knowing how to use the application will help you to manage your workflow effectively.

TOPIC A

Identify the Components of the Outlook Interface

You may have used other email applications or services. Before you work with Outlook, you want to familiarize yourself with its environment. In this topic, you will identify the components of the Outlook 2010 user interface.

Becoming familiar with the user interface of any application is essential to start using it. When working with any new software, you could potentially waste a significant amount of time searching for specific options in the environment. You can prevent this by identifying the interface elements and some of the options provided. This basic knowledge will help you achieve the results that you are seeking when you begin using the software.

Microsoft Office Outlook 2010

Outlook is a mail application that is part of the Microsoft Office suite. It is used to communicate with others electronically, by sending and receiving email messages. With Outlook, you can also schedule meetings and tasks, and perform various other communication and organization functions, such as managing personal information.

The Microsoft Office Outlook 2010 Window

The Microsoft Office Outlook 2010 window has a variety of interface components.

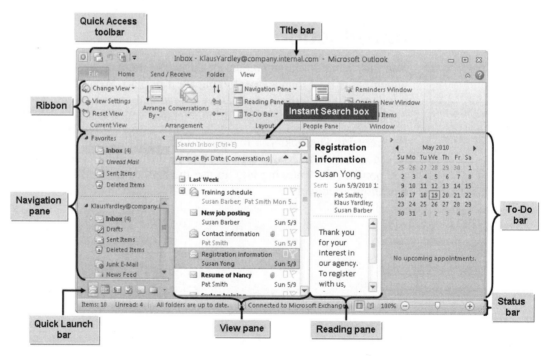

Figure 1-1: The Outlook window and its various interface components.

Component	Description
Title bar	Located at the top of the application window, it displays the name of the current folder, the email account, and the application.
Navigation pane	Located on the left side of the application window, it provides access to most items and folders of Outlook. It can be minimized and customized.
Quick Access toolbar	Located above the Ribbon to the left of the title bar, it provides easy access to many commands in the application. The Quick Access toolbar can also be placed below the Ribbon, and can be customized to include other commands, based on the user's preferences and requirements.
Ribbon	Located below the title bar, it provides access to application commands.
View pane	Placed immediately to the right of the Navigation pane, it lists all email messages that can be viewed.
Reading pane	Located on the right side of the View pane, it displays the content of a selected message. The content of the message is displayed as a preview before the message is opened.
Quick Launch bar	Located below the Navigation pane, it provides quick access to frequently used items and folders. It can be used to switch to different item views.
Instant Search box	Located at the top of the View pane, it allows you to enter search terms and locate related content across different items.
To-Do bar	Located on the right side of the Reading pane, it displays the calendar, upcoming appointments, and flagged messages. You can use the To-Do bar to organize and manage your priorities. It can be customized to display only the required information.
Status bar	Located at the bottom of the application window, it displays information about the active folder.

The Ribbon

The *Ribbon* is a component at the top of the user interface, below the title bar, that holds sets of easily accessed commands, providing you with quick access to task-specific commands. Commands that are relevant to any particular task are located together on a tab that represents the functionality of those commands. The Ribbon can be customized by adding or removing tabs, groups, and individual commands. You can also hide the Ribbon by double-clicking an active tab.

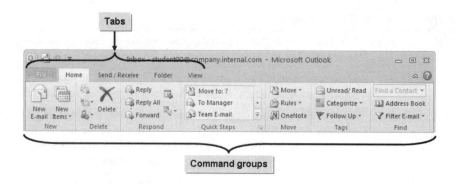

Figure 1-2: The Ribbon displaying the tabs and command groups on the Home tab.

The Ribbon Tabs

The Ribbon tabs allow you to access commands that perform simple or advanced operations without having to navigate extensively.

Ribbon Tab	Used To
File	Access various commands such as **Save As, Save Attachments, Info, Open, Print, Help, Options,** and **Exit.** It also displays an interface called the Backstage view with commands to perform additional tasks such as to change account settings and manage your files and data stored in the application.
Home	Access different sets of commands and options available for various items in the application. The commands and options displayed on the **Home** tab vary for different items such as mail messages, calendars, and contacts.
Send/Receive	Send and receive messages, appointments, meetings and calendars. You can also use these commands to work offline and to control the downloading of messages and items.
Folder	Create, rename and move folders. You can also use these commands to clean up unwanted content in the folders, mark folders as favorites and archive them for future reference.
View	View items with your preferred setting. You can choose a preferred setting to view and arrange items and specify layout preferences to customize the display of items and folders in Outlook.

ScreenTips

ScreenTips are small windows of descriptive text that are displayed when the mouse pointer is placed over a command or a button. The descriptive text provides you with hints about the functions that you can perform using the particular component.

The Backstage View

The Backstage view is displayed when you select the **File** tab. Containing a series of tabs that group similar commands, the Backstage view displays various Outlook options that are used to manage data stored in the application. This view also simplifies access to Outlook features, and lets you save, modify account settings, open calendars and data files, print items, display the **Outlook Options** dialog box and exit the application with a few mouse clicks. By default, when the Backstage view is launched, the **Account Information** page is displayed that allows you to set account information, such as adding accounts and sending automatic replies.

Figure 1-3: The Backstage view displaying the Account Information page.

Dialog Box Launchers

Dialog box launchers are small buttons with a downward pointing arrow located at the bottom-right corner of certain command groups on a tab. They are used to launch dialog boxes with commands that are specific to the features found in that group, and are used to adjust the settings that are not available on the Ribbon.

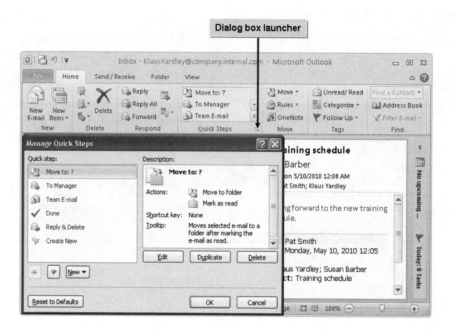

Figure 1-4: A dialog box launcher opens a dialog box.

Items and Folders

The basic element in Outlook is an item. Items hold information and include mail messages, calendars, contacts, tasks, and notes.

A *folder* is a container that is used to store Outlook items. Folders can be created, moved, and grouped to organize items so that they can be easily accessed. Separate folders can be created to store information categorically, and can be displayed in the Navigation pane. Folders can be organized for easy retrieval of mail messages and information regarding meetings and appointments. Some folders are available as defaults, and include the Deleted Items, Inbox, and Sent Items folders.

The Inbox

The Inbox is a folder that is displayed in the Navigation pane, and that stores the user's email messages. The contents of the Inbox are displayed in the View pane. The Inbox may contain mail messages and meeting requests that are received by the user. By default, the Inbox is the active folder when Outlook is launched.

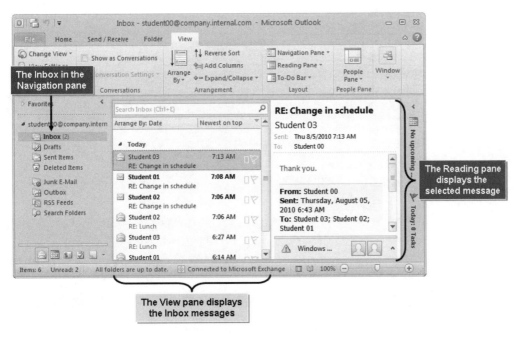

Figure 1-5: The Inbox displaying messages in the View pane.

Additional Folders in Outlook

Additional folders in Outlook include:

- Deleted Items: Stores any item that you delete from Outlook.
- Drafts: Stores copies of unfinished messages, which you can complete and send later.
- Junk E-mail: Contains junk email messages.
- Outbox: Temporarily stores the outgoing messages until they are delivered.
- Sent Items: Stores copies of messages that you sent to others.
- Sync Issues: Contains all the synchronization logs.
- Search Folders: Contains views of mail items that satisfy specific search criteria.

Outlook Help

Outlook Help is a repository of information about the functionality of various features of Microsoft Outlook 2010. The Outlook Help window provides a quick and easy way to find answers to Outlook-related queries, online or offline. You can access information by browsing through the links that are already given or by performing keyword-based searches.

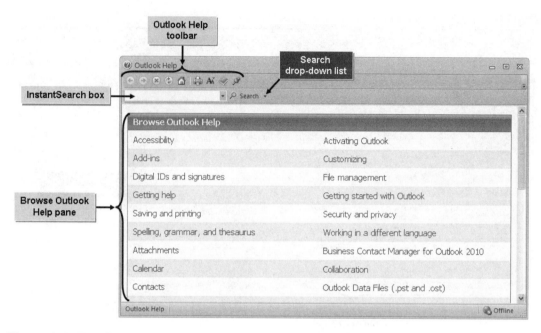

Figure 1-6: The Outlook Help window displaying links to information.

The Outlook Help window provides a number of options that allow you to find answers to all your Outlook-related queries.

Option	Description
The **Outlook Help** toolbar	Provides access to navigation, print, and format commands.
The **Type words to search for** text box	Allows you to type the keyword on which you need to search for information. Previously used keywords can be found in the **Search Criteria** drop-down list.
The **Search** drop-down list	Provides options based on the criterion that you have chosen to search for information from online or offline content.
The **Browse Outlook Help** pane	Displays the topics available in Outlook Help in a tabular format. You can navigate to a topic by clicking it.

Outlook Help Toolbar Options

On the Outlook Help toolbar, there are buttons that enable you to navigate through Outlook Help. You can move back and forth between pages, stop a search that is in progress, display the Help Home page or the table of contents, or print a particular Help topic. You can also control the appearance of information by increasing or decreasing the size of the text or by setting the Help window to stay on top of other windows.

Button	Used To
Back	Navigate to the page that was previously accessed.

Button	Used To
Forward	Navigate to the next page. The **Forward** button is enabled only after the **Back** button has been used.
Stop	Stop the search that is in progress.
Refresh	Refresh the page that is currently displayed.
Home	Display the Home page of Outlook Help.
Print	Print a Help page with specific options.
Change Font Size	Increase or decrease the font size of the text in a Help topic.
Show Table of Contents	Display the task pane, which contains the table of contents of Outlook Help.
Keep On Top/Not On Top	Position the Outlook Help window on top of the other windows of Microsoft Outlook. By clicking the **Keep On Top** button, you can toggle to the **Not On Top** button. The **Not On Top** button is used to position the other Outlook windows on top of the Outlook Help window.

Wildcard Characters

A *wildcard* is a special symbol that can represent one or more characters in a search keyword. For example, the asterisk symbol (*) is a wildcard that stands for any combination of letters. However, Outlook Help does not qualify wildcard characters as searchable text.

Areas of Search in Outlook Help

In Outlook Help, you can specify the area of search to narrow down the search results. Areas of search can be either online or offline. You can access **Outlook Help** and **Developer Reference** from either **Content from Office.com** or **Content from this computer.**

Area Of Search	Provides
All Outlook	Information on the keyword from the built-in Help and takes you to the Office online website, if required.
Outlook Help	Information on the keyword from the built-in Help as well as the Office online website, but does not take you to the Office online website.
Outlook Templates	Information on sample templates that is available on the Office online website.
Outlook Training	Sample training information from the Office online website.
Developer Reference	Information on programing tasks, samples, and references to create customized solutions.

ACTIVITY 1-1
Exploring the Outlook Environment

Scenario:
Before you begin using Outlook, it is a good idea to spend some time familiarizing yourself with the Outlook interface components.

1. Launch Outlook and view its items.

    a. Choose **Start** →**All Programs** →Microsoft Office→Microsoft Outlook 2010.

    b. In the **Security Alert** message box, click **Yes.**

    c. In the **Security Alert** message box which appears again, click **Yes.**

    > If the PC is set up for multiple users, you can use the **Profile Name** drop-down list box in the **Choose Profile** dialog box to select a user.

    d. Below the Navigation pane, on the Quick Launch bar, click **Calendar** to view the Outlook calendar.

    e. On the Quick Launch bar, click **Contacts** to view the contacts with whom you will communicate.

    f. On the Quick Launch bar, click the **Folder list** button to view all the folders in the Navigation pane.

2. Display the contents of other folders.

    a. In the Navigation pane, in the **Favorites** section, click the black arrow to collapse the **Favorites** section.

    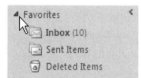

b. In the Navigation pane, click the Sent Items folder to view the email messages that were sent to contacts.

c. Click the Deleted Items folder to view an email that was deleted.

3. Explore the other interface elements.

   a. On the Ribbon, observe the **File, Home, Send / Receive, Folder,** and **View** tabs.

   b. On the Quick Access toolbar, click the **Customize Quick Access Toolbar** drop-down arrow, located third from the left, to display the options in the drop-down list.

   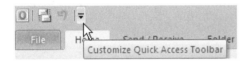

   c. Observe the options in the drop-down list and click the **Customize Quick Access Toolbar** drop-down arrow to close the drop-down list.

4. Explore the **Home** tab for mail items.

   a. On the Ribbon, verify that the **Home** tab is selected.

   b. In the **New** group, place the mouse pointer over the **New E-mail** button to view the ScreenTip that displays a description and the shortcut key for this command.

   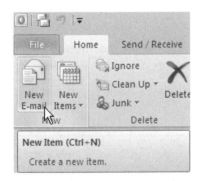

   c. In the **Find** group, place the mouse pointer over the **Address Book** button to display the ScreenTip to view the button command.

    The **Address Book** button can be used to open the address book, and the shortcut key to launch the address book.

5. Explore the changes on the **Home** tab for other items in Outlook.

   a. On the Quick Launch bar, click **Calendar.**

   b. Observe that the groups and commands on the **Home** tab have changed to calendar options.

   c. On the Quick Launch bar, click **Contacts.**

   d. Observe that the groups and commands on the **Home** tab have changed to contacts options.

6. Display the **Go To Date** dialog box and minimize the Ribbon.

   a. On the Quick Launch bar, click **Calendar.**

   b. On the **Home** tab, in the **Go To** group, click the **Go to Date** dialog box launcher.

   c. In the **Go To Date** dialog box, click **Cancel** to close it.

   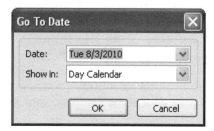

   d. At the top-right corner of the Ribbon, click the **Minimize the Ribbon** button, located second from the right, to minimize the Ribbon.

   e. Observe that the Ribbon is collapsed with only the tabs displayed and that there is additional workspace available in the window.

   f. Click the **Expand the Ribbon** button to maximize the Ribbon.

7. Launch the Outlook Help window.

   a. In the Outlook window, click the **Help** button, located on the top-right corner of the window above the Ribbon.

   b. Observe that the Outlook Help window is displayed.

   c. In the Outlook Help window, on the title bar, click the **Maximize** button to maximize the window.

8. Search for information relating to calendars.

    a. In the Outlook Help window, in the **Type words to search for** text box, click and type *calendar* and then press **Enter**.

    > calendar

    b. Observe that topics that contain information relating to calendars are displayed in the Outlook Help window.

9. Search for information through the table of contents.

    a. On the Outlook Help toolbar, click the **Show Table of Contents** button, located second from right, to display the table of contents.

    b. In the **Table of Contents** pane, click the **Getting help** link to display its contents.

    c. Below the **Getting help** link, click the **What and where is the Backstage view** link to view information about the Backstage view.

    d. Observe the information about the Backstage view and click the **Close** button to close the **Table of Contents** pane.

    e. On the Outlook Help toolbar, click the **Home** button, to display the Help Home page.

10. Retain the Outlook Help window on top of the other windows.

    a. In the Outlook Help window, click the **Restore Down** button to restore the window to its original size.

    b. On the Outlook Help toolbar, place the mouse pointer over the first button from the right, the **Keep On Top** button, to view its ScreenTip.

    c. In the Outlook window, click to the right of the Quick Access toolbar.

d. Observe that the Outlook Help window is displayed on top even after selecting the Outlook window. Close the Outlook Help window.

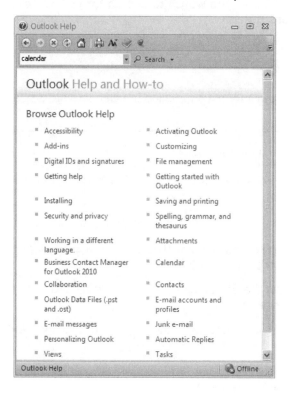

TOPIC B
Read an Email Message

You are familiar with the components of the Outlook 2010 application window. You now want to use the application to read messages that you receive. In this topic, you will read an email message that you received.

It is important that you open and read the email message to know the content of the message and the information conveyed to you by the sender. By using Outlook, you can read email messages and also ensure effective communication of important events or information.

Email

Definition:

An *email* is a message that is sent electronically using a standard email application. An email message is written in a format that is similar to the one used to draft letters. It is drafted by the sender and is sent to the intended recipient. It can contain information in the form of text or images. It can also carry information in the form of attached files. Email messages are composed, sent, and received using email applications.

Example:

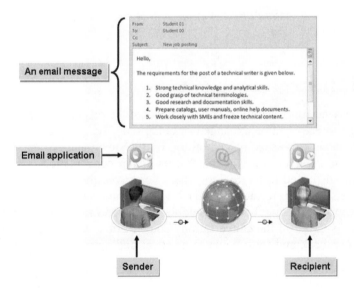

Figure 1-7: An email message sent electronically using an email application.

The AutoPreview Feature

The *AutoPreview* feature enables you to preview the first few lines of a message in the View pane, without actually opening the message. When you click once on the unopened email, a portion of the message content is displayed beneath the subject line of the message. Outlook allows you to hide or display the preview.

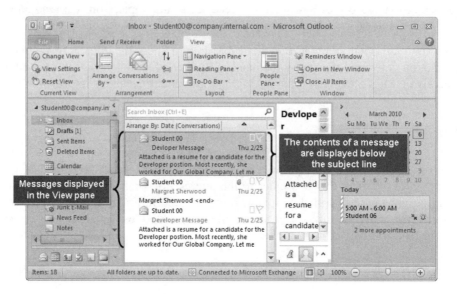

Figure 1-8: The AutoPreview feature displaying the first few lines of a message in the View pane.

Conversations

In Outlook, email messages that share the same subject can be displayed together as a *Conversation*. These message threads can be expanded or collapsed. The messages in a conversation are arranged with the newest message placed on top in the View pane. When there is a response to the email in a conversation thread, that particular conversation is also moved to the top. Conversations are displayed in the folders where you saved the messages even if some messages in the conversation are located in other folders. Conversations are identified with an icon of multiple envelopes. The number of envelopes displayed in the icon corresponds to the number of messages displayed in the conversation. Conversations are useful when multiple communications happen back and forth between a sender and a receiver.

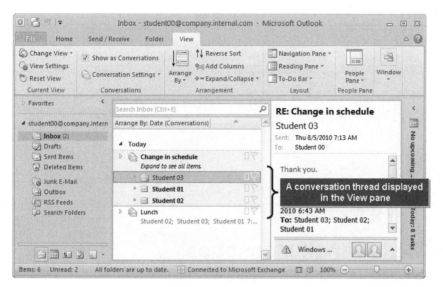

Figure 1-9: A conversation thread displaying messages that share the same subject.

Split Conversation

A conversation thread that has more than one message thread is called a split conversation. This may occur when an individual replies to an earlier message in a conversation rather than the latest message.

Conversation Symbols

The grey and orange symbols shown to the left of each message indicate the status of a message in a conversation. An orange dot identifies the latest message in a message thread and also helps identify the number of specific message threads in the conversation. A small orange square identifies the message that immediately precedes the selected message. A small gray square identifies all other messages that belong to the selected message thread.

Message Symbols

Each message in your Inbox displays one or more symbols next to it. The symbols represent the type or status of the message.

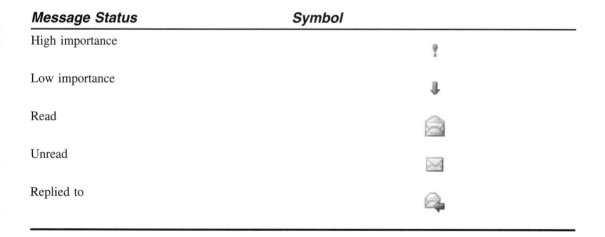

Message Status	Symbol
Forwarded	
Attachment	
For follow-up	
Complete	

How to Read Email Messages

Procedure Reference: Preview a Message Automatically

To preview a message automatically:

1. In the Navigation pane, select **Inbox.**
2. If necessary, in the View pane, in the Inbox, select the desired message.
3. On the Ribbon, select the **View** tab.
4. On the **View** tab, in the **Current View** group, click **View Settings** to set the AutoPreview feature.
5. In the **Advanced View Settings : Compact** dialog box, click the **Other Settings** button.
6. In the **Other Settings** dialog box, in the **AutoPreview** section, select the desired options.
   - Click **Preview all items** to preview all the messages that are present in the Inbox.
   - Click **Preview unread items** to preview only the unread messages.
   - Click **No AutoPreview** to disable the AutoPreview feature.

Procedure Reference: Open a Message

To open a message:

1. Open a message from the View pane.
   - Double-click the message you want to open or;
   - Right-click the message you want to open and choose **Open** or;
   - Select the message you want to open and press **Enter.**
2. Close the message window after reading it.

Procedure Reference: Customize the Reading Pane

To customize the Reading pane:

1. In the Navigation pane, select the **Inbox.**
2. In the View pane, select a message to view it in the Reading pane.

3. Select the **View** tab, and in the **Layout** group, from the **Reading Pane** drop-down list, select an option to relocate the Reading pane.
   - Select **Bottom** to move the Reading pane to the bottom of the Outlook window.
   - Select **Off** to hide the Reading pane.
   - Select **Right** to move the Reading pane to the right side of the Outlook window.

Procedure Reference: View Messages as a Conversation

To view messages as a conversation:
1. Select messages that you want to view as a conversation.
2. View the messages as a conversation.
   - On the **View** tab, in the **Conversations** group, check the **Show as Conversations** check box.
   - On the **View** tab, in the **Conversations** group, click the **Conversation Settings** drop-down arrow and select the desired option to view the messages as a conversation.
     - Select **Show Messages from Other Folders** to show selected messages from other folders as part of the conversation.
     - Select **Show Senders Above the Subject** to show the name of the sender above the subject of the message in the View pane.
     - Select **Always Expand Conversations** to display all messages in the conversation.
     - Select **Use Classic Indented View** to view conversation by hierarchy in which messages are indented to show you who replied to whom and when they replied.

ACTIVITY 1-2
Reading Messages

Scenario:
Before you take action on any messages, you want to customize the Reading pane and enable message previews. Then you need to read the message sent by your manager detailing the new training schedule. In addition, there are some responses to this message and you want to view all the individual message threads to quickly decide on your response to all the senders. Also, you do not want all the email messages in this thread to be displayed, as there are already too many email messages in the View pane.

1. View messages as a conversation.

    a. On the Quick Launch bar, click **Mail** and select Inbox.

    b. Select the **View** tab, and in the **Conversations** group, check the **Show as conversation** check box.

    c. In the **Microsoft Outlook** message box, click **This folder** to display messages in the Inbox as conversations.

    d. In the View pane, select the **Training schedule** message.

    e. In the View pane, click the arrow at the left of the **Training schedule message** to expand it.

    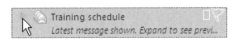

    f. Observe that the conversation displays three messages.

    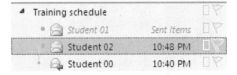

2. Specify settings to preview messages in the View pane.

    a. On the **View** tab, in the **Current View** group, click **View Settings**.

b. In the **Advanced View Settings: Compact** dialog box, click **Other Settings.**

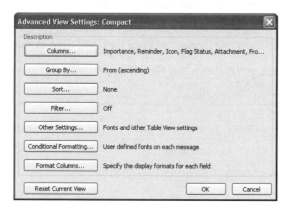

c. In the **Other Settings** dialog box, in the **AutoPreview** section, select the **Preview all items** option and click **OK.**

d. In the **Advanced View Settings : Compact** dialog box, click **OK.**

e. Observe that the messages in the View pane display a few lines of the message as a preview.

3. Hide the Reading pane.

   a. Verify that the content of the latest message in the Training schedule conversation is displayed in the Reading pane.

   b. On the **View** tab, in the **Layout** group, from the **Reading Pane** drop-down list, select **Off** to hide the Reading pane.

   c. Observe that the View pane is displayed in the entire window.

4. Open the Training schedule message.

   a. In the View pane, click the arrow at the left of the Training schedule message to view all the messages in the conversation.

   b. Verify that a symbol with multiple envelopes is placed to the left of the message header.

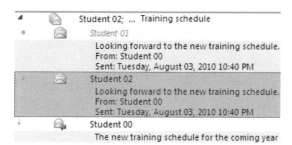

   c. In the **View** pane, double-click the selected **Training schedule** message to open it.

   d. Read the message and click the **Close** button to close it.

5. View messages as individual messages and restore the reading pane.

a. On the **View** tab, in the **Conversations** group, uncheck the **Show as Conversations** check box, and in the Microsoft Outlook message box, click the **This folder.**

b. In the View pane, observe that the mail messages in the Training schedule conversation are displayed as individual mail messages and not grouped as a conversation.

c. On the **View** tab, in the **Layout** group, from the **Reading pane** drop-down list, select **Right** to restore the Reading pane.

TOPIC C
Reply to and Forward an Email Message

You read an email message. The sender of the email may expect a reply from you or you may want to send an email to others. In this topic, you will respond to email messages.

Often you may need to respond to email messages to convey information or inform others about your availability for appointments, agendas, or proposals. You may also have to share important information that you receive with others in your team or with clients and stakeholders. The ability to reply to email messages that you receive lets you quickly convey important information to others.

Message Reply Options

Outlook provides you with various options for responding to email messages. The buttons in the **Respond** group on the **Message** tab allow you to choose the type of response that is most appropriate.

Figure 1-10: Reply options in the Respond group on the Message tab.

Button	Allows You To
Reply	Compose an email to the sender, in response to the email received.
Reply All	Compose an email in response to the sender, with a copy to all who received the original email message.
Forward	Forward an email message to chosen contacts.
Meeting	Create a meeting request when you reply to an email.
More Respond Actions	Forward an email as an attachment or as a text message.

The InfoBar

The *InfoBar* displays information about what has occurred or what action you need to perform in the mail box. It is displayed below the Ribbon and has details such as the status of the email.

Message Forwards

Outlook allows you to *forward* email messages to any number of email recipients, provided they have a valid email address in any of the **To, Cc,** or **Bcc** fields. After an email is forwarded, the email symbol in Outlook changes to a forward arrow symbol.

Mail Tracking Options

Mail tracking options in Outlook help you confirm whether a recipient has received or read the email that you sent. You can add tracking to email messages to follow actions that result from communication through email messages. Requests for delivery and read receipts can be enabled for you to keep track of when the email was delivered and when it was read. This helps you confirm that the message is read by the intended recipient.

Figure 1-11: Options to track email displayed in the Tracking group on the Options tab.

Outlook provides various mail tracking options.

Option	Provides
Use Voting Buttons	Options to take a simple yes or no poll or add custom voting buttons. Results are tracked and counted.
Request a Delivery Receipt	Notifications when a message is delivered.
Request a Read Receipt	Notifications when a message is read by the recipient.

How to Reply to and Forward a Message

Procedure Reference: Reply to a Message

To reply to a message:

1. If necessary, open a received message.
2. Reply to the message.
   - On the **Message** tab of the Message form, in the **Respond** group, click **Reply** to reply only to the sender of the message or;
   - Click **Reply All** to reply to the sender and to all the recipients of the message.

You do not have to open a message to reply to it. Select the message in the Inbox and on the Ribbon, click **Reply**.

The **To** and **Subject** text boxes are automatically filled in and information from the original message is inserted in the message body.

3. In the message body, type the text of the message and send the message.
4. If necessary, close the original message.

Procedure Reference: Forward a Message

To forward a message:

1. In the View pane, select or open the message that is to be forwarded.
2. Forward the message.
   - On the **Message** tab, in the **Respond** group, click **Forward** or;
   - On the **Home** tab, in the **Respond** group, click **Forward**.
3. In the **To** text box, enter the name of the recipient and click **Send** to forward the message.
4. If necessary, close the original message.

ACTIVITY 1-3
Replying to and Forwarding a Message

Scenario:
The message from a coworker contains the job description for the Technical Writer position. After reading the job description, you feel that you have a few candidates suitable for the position. You need to inform your coworker about them. You also want your manager's opinion on the qualification requirement of a candidate, so you will forward an email to your manager.

1. Reply to the New job posting message.

    a. In the View pane, double-click the **New job posting** message that you received from your partner.

    b. Maximize the New job posting - Message (HTML) window.

    c. In the New job posting - Message (HTML) window, on the **Message** tab, in the **Respond** group, click **Reply.**

    d. Maximize the RE:New job posting - Message (HTML) window,

    e. In the message body, type *The job description is perfect. I have some candidates for the position.* Click **Send.**

2. Forward the New job posting message to your manager.

    a. In the New job posting - Message (HTML) window, on the **Message** tab, in the **Respond** group, click **Forward.**

    b. In the FW: New job posting - Message (HTML) window, in the **To** text box, type *student00* and press **Tab.**

    c. In the message body, click and type *I received this job description and am working on selecting a few candidates to fill the position.* Click **Send.**

    d. Close the original message.

TOPIC D
Print an Email Message

You responded to messages in Outlook. Although email is primarily a form of electronic communication, there may be occasions when you want to have a hard copy of a message. In this topic, you will print an email message.

There may be times when you do not have access to Outlook, or even a computer, but still need to have the information that you received by email on hand. It will be helpful if you can have a hard copy of the information. Printing a copy of the message provides you with a handy reference to refer to when needed.

The Print Dialog Box

The **Print** dialog box allows you to specify print settings to output Outlook items on a printer. The **Print** dialog box can be used to print an item with the default print settings or to customize the print settings for print quality. The different sections and options in the **Print** dialog box allow you to perform various functions like choosing a printer, selecting the number of copies to print with the selected page numbers, and specifying the form in which mail messages are to be printed.

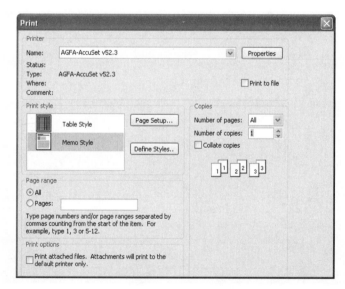

Figure 1-12: The Print dialog box displaying options for printing an Outlook item.

How to Print an Email Message

Procedure Reference: Print an Email Message

To print an email message:

1. Open the message you want to print.
2. Select the **File** tab and choose **Print.**
3. In the Backstage view, click **Print Options** to display the **Print** dialog box.
4. Select the desired print options.
   - In the **Printer** section, from the **Name** drop-down list, select a printer.
   - In the **Print Style** section, select the desired print style.
   - In the **Page range** section, specify the pages you want to print.
     - Select **All** to print all pages.
     - Select **Pages** and in the **Pages** text box specify the pages you want to print.
   - In the **Copies** section, specify the number of copies to be printed.
     - In the **Number of pages** drop-down list select an option.
     - In the **Number of copies** spin box select an option.
5. Click **OK** to print the message and close the message.

ACTIVITY 1-4
Printing a Message

Scenario:
The email with the job description for a Technical Writer is stored in your Inbox. You are going to interview three candidates for the position, and you want to distribute a copy of the description to each candidate, plus have a printed copy for yourself.

1. Display the **Print** dialog box.

    a. In the View pane, verify that the New job posting message is selected.

    b. On the Ribbon, select the **File** tab and choose **Print.**

    c. In the Backstage view, in the **Printer** section, click **Print Options** to display the **Print** dialog box.

2. Print four copies of the message.

    a. In the **Print** dialog box, in the **Printer** section, from the **Name** drop-down list, select a printer.

    b. In the **Copies** section, in the **Number of copies** spin box, click the up arrow three times to set the number of copies to be printed as 4.

    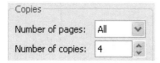

    c. Click **Print** to print the message.

TOPIC E
Delete an Email Message

You printed an email message. As you regularly use Outlook to communicate, your Inbox could quickly fill up with messages, some of them that you no longer need. In this topic, you will delete unwanted email messages.

Keeping the email messages you need and removing those that you do not require is one of the most important challenges you will face with the large amount of email messages that can flood your Inbox. When you have a lot of email communication, it is difficult to retain all messages that were part of the communication because some of them may not be essential after a point in time. By deleting unwanted messages, your Inbox will be less cluttered, making it easier to find an email message when you need it.

The Auto Empty Feature

When you delete an email message from the Inbox, it is moved to the Deleted Items folder, and you have to manually delete each item from the Deleted Items folder to permanently delete them. If you want to delete all items automatically, then you can enable the Auto Empty feature, which will empty the Deleted Items folder when you exit Outlook.

Figure 1-13: The Outlook Options dialog box displaying the settings to remove messages from the Deleted Items folder.

How to Delete an Email Message

Procedure Reference: Delete a Message

To delete a message:

1. In the Navigation pane, select the folder from which you want to delete a message.
2. Delete a message.
    - Delete a message displayed in the View pane.
        a. In the View pane, select the message that needs to be deleted.
        b. On the **Home** tab, in the **Delete** group, click **Delete.**
    - Open a message, and delete it.
        a. In the View pane, double-click the message to open it.
        b. On the **Message** tab, in the **Delete** group, click **Delete** to delete the message.
3. If necessary, in the Navigation pane, verify that the message is deleted, by clicking the Deleted Items folder.

Procedure Reference: Recover Deleted Messages

To recover a deleted message:

1. In the Navigation pane, select the Deleted Items folder.
2. Select the messages that you want to recover.
3. Drag the messages from the Deleted Items folder to any other folder in the Navigation pane.

Procedure Reference: Delete Messages Permanently

To delete messages permanently:

1. In the Navigation pane, select the Deleted Items folder to view the deleted messages.
2. Delete messages.
    - Delete the messages manually.
        a. In the Deleted Items folder, select the messages to be deleted permanently.
            - Right-click the selected messages and choose **Delete** to delete the messages permanently or;
            - Open the messages and on the **Home** tab, in the **Delete** group, click **Delete.**
        b. In the **Microsoft Outlook** dialog box, click **Yes** to delete the messages manually.
    - Delete the messages automatically.
        a. Select the **File** tab and choose **Options** to display the **Outlook Options** dialog box.
        b. In the **Outlook Options** dialog box, select the **Advanced** tab.
        c. In the **Outlook start and exit** section, check the **Empty Deleted Items folder when exiting Outlook** check box and click **OK** to close the **Outlook Options** dialog box.
        d. If necessary, close the Outlook application, and in the **Microsoft Office Outlook** message box, click **Yes** to permanently delete the messages from the Deleted Items folder.

ACTIVITY 1-5
Deleting Messages

Scenario:
The vacancy for the Technical Writer position is now closed. You no longer need the message that contains the job description. Because you find it tedious to manually clear the deleted items from the Deleted Items folder, you decide to automate the process.

1. Delete the New job posting message.

   a. Select the **Home** tab, and in the **Delete** group, click **Delete.**

   b. In the Navigation pane, in the **student##@company.internal.com** section, select the Deleted Items folder.

   c. Observe that the New job posting message is displayed in the Deleted Items folder.

2. Delete the message permanently by the manual method.

   a. In the View pane, verify that the New job posting message is selected.

   b. On the **Home** tab, in the **Delete** group, click **Delete.**

   c. In the **Microsoft Outlook** message box, click **Yes** to confirm deletion of the message.

   d. Observe that the New job posting message is no longer displayed in the Deleted Items folder.

3. Set the automatic option for deletion of messages permanently.

   a. On the Ribbon, select the **File** tab and choose **Options** to display the **Outlook Options** dialog box.

   b. In the **Outlook Options** dialog box, select the **Advanced** tab.

   c. In the **Outlook start and exit** section, check the **Empty Deleted Items folder when exiting Outlook** check box and click **OK** to set the automatic option to delete a message permanently when closing the Outlook application.

Lesson 1 Follow-up

In this lesson, you identified the basic components of Outlook and used the application to read and respond to messages. Familiarity with the tools and working with basic email-related tasks enable you to use Outlook effectively.

1. **According to you, which is the most useful feature in the Outlook 2010 environment? Why?**

2. **Which feature would you prefer to use when viewing messages? Why?**

2 Composing Messages

Lesson Time: 1 hour(s), 15 minutes

Lesson Objectives:

In this lesson, you will compose email messages.

You will:
- Create an email message.
- Format an email message.
- Check the spelling and grammar in email messages.
- Attach a file to an email message.
- Use contextual tabs.
- Send an email message.

Introduction

You used Outlook to work with messages that you received. The next logical step will be to compose and send an email message. In this lesson, you will compose email messages by using Outlook.

Email messaging plays an indispensible role in business communication. Using Outlook, you can compose email messages based on your requirements. Besides composing an email message, you can also format it, and include additional information in the form of attachments. Formatting a message allows you to emphasize text within the body of the message, and correcting any misspelled words before sending it ensures that your message is both accurate and easy to read.

TOPIC A
Create an Email Message

Now that you are familiar with the Outlook environment, you are ready to communicate with others using the application. In this topic, you will create an email message.

In its basic form, composing email is a matter of writing a clear and concise message in the body of the email form, and addressing it correctly. When your recipients can clearly understand the purpose of your message, they can take the proper action or respond appropriately. An effective email goes a long way in helping people communicate better.

Email Addresses

Definition:

An *email address* is a string that specifies the recipient's user name and domain name. The user name is followed by the @ symbol, and a domain name that includes a period and an extension such as .com, .net, or other standard extensions. The user name is unique to every email address within a given domain, and is made up of alphabetic and/or numeric characters. It may also have other characters such as periods and underscores.

Example:

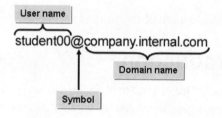

Figure 2-1: An email address string specifying the user name and domain name.

The Address Book

The *address book* is a collection of information about contacts. A contact is a person with whom you intend to communicate. You can use the address book to find and select the names of contacts, email addresses, and distribution lists to quickly address messages. It not only stores all addresses in one location for easy access but also contains the names and addresses of specific users and groups. The address book can also include other business and personal information such as physical addresses and phone numbers.

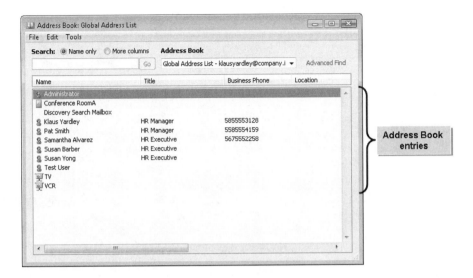

Figure 2-2: An address book displaying a list of contacts.

Microsoft Exchange Server

Microsoft Exchange Server is a mail server application that is used to manage email messages in a network. It serves as a central communication platform through which users can communicate with their contacts to share schedules, meetings, and other important information. Outlook can be connected to a network of computers through the Microsoft Exchange Server.

Global Address Lists

A *Global Address List* is a list of all user names and distribution lists in an organization created and maintained by the Microsoft Exchange Server administrator. You can only access the *Global Address List* if you are using a Microsoft Exchange Server email account. It provides information on different resources that are available for conducting meetings and conferences scheduled through Outlook.

The Message Form

The Message form is a window that allows you to compose, send, reply to, and forward email messages. The Message form is launched by clicking the **New Email** button in the **New** group on the **Home** tab. The Message form displays a different Ribbon with tabs that provide options you can use to compose and format email messages. The Message form displays the **To** and **Cc** text boxes for you to fill in email addresses of the recipients. By default, the **Bcc** text box is not displayed. The Message form allows you to enter the subject of the mail in the **Subject** text box. The message body is where you will type in your message.

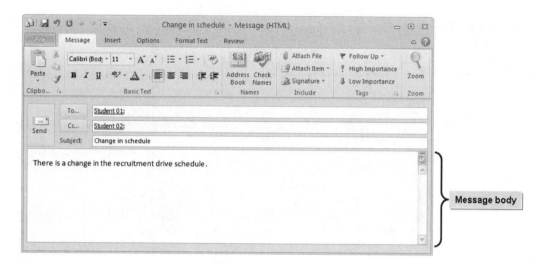

Figure 2-3: The message form in Outlook.

Message Form Tabs

In Outlook, the tabs that are displayed on the Ribbon differ for each form. The Message form has tabs that contain commands and options used to create messages.

Tab	Description
Message	Displayed on the Ribbon of the Message form. It provides common options to format text, attach files and items, append signatures, and set follow-up options and priorities for an email message.
Insert	Displayed on the Ribbon of the Message, Appointment, Meeting, Contact, and Tasks forms. It provides options to insert different objects such as files, charts, tables, symbols, and pictures that can be added to a message while drafting it.
Options	Displayed on the Ribbon of the Message form. It provides various options to enhance the appearance of your email, modify message delivery options, as well as include different fields in the message.
Format Text	Displayed on the Ribbon of the Message, Appointment, Meeting, Contact, and Task forms. It contains the most commonly used options for formatting text and changing styles.
Review	Displayed on the Ribbon of the Message, Appointment, Meeting, Contact, and Task forms. It contains the commonly used commands for reviewing content, along with proofing options.

How to Create an Email Message

Procedure Reference: Compose a Message Using the Message Form

To compose a message using the Message form:

1. Launch the Outlook application.
2. Display a new Message form.
   - On the **Home** tab, in the **New** group, click **New E-mail** or;
   - In the **New** group, from the **New Items** drop-down list, select **E-Mail Message.**
3. In the Message form, enter the necessary details.
   - In the **To** text box, type the recipient's email address.
   - If necessary, in the **Cc** text box, type the recipient's email address that is to receive a copy.
   - In the **Subject** text box, type the subject of the message.
   - In the message body, type the content of the message.

Procedure Reference: Create a Message Using the Global Address List

To create a message using the **Global Address List:**

1. Display a new Message form.
2. In the Message form, click **To** to display the **Select Names: Global Address List** dialog box.
3. In the **Select Names: Global Address List** dialog box, in the list box, click **Names only** to display the names of contacts.
4. Select the user name of the person to whom you want to address the message.
5. In the section below the list box, click **To** to place the user name in the **To** text box and click **OK.**
6. In the Message form, enter the necessary details and click **OK.**

Procedure Reference: Create a Message Using the Contacts List in the Address Book

To create a message using the contacts list in the Address Book:

1. Display a new Message form.
2. On the **Home** tab, in the **Names** group, click **Address Book** to display the **Select Names** dialog box.
3. In the **Select Names** dialog box, from the **Address Book** drop-down list, select **Contacts.**
4. Select the user name of the person to whom you want to address the message.
5. In the section below the list box, click **To** to place the user name in the **To** text box and click **OK.**
6. In the Message form, enter the necessary details and click **Send** to send the message.

ACTIVITY 2-1
Creating an Email Message

Scenario:

You want a coworker to review a resume. You have to first locate her email address and then compose the message.

1. Use the **Global Address List** to address a new message to your partner.

    a. In the Navigation pane, in the **student##company.internal.com** section, select the **Inbox**.

    b. Verify that the View pane displays the messages in the **Inbox** and that the content of the selected message is displayed in the **Reading** pane.

    c. On the **Home** tab, in the **New** group, click **New E-mail** to open a new Message form.

    d. In the Untitled - Message (HTML) window, click **To.**

    e. In the **Select Names: Global Address List** dialog box, in the **Search** section, verify that the **Name only** option is selected.

    f. In the list box, select your partner's user name and click **To** to insert it in the **To** text box.

    g. Click **OK** to insert the user name in the Message form.

2. Enter the subject and message body for the email.

     Note that the text has a misspelled word "postion" and a typographical error showing no space between the words *workingfor,* which will be corrected in a subsequent activity.

    a. In the **Subject** text box, click and type *Developer position*

    b. Click in the message body, type *Hello* and then press **Enter** twice.

    c. Type *Attached is a resume of a candidate for the Developer postion. Most recently, she is workingfor 3Rz Learning.* Press **Enter** twice.

    d. Type *Let me know your thoughts by tomorrow.* Press **Enter** twice.

    e. In the message body, type *Regards*

TOPIC B
Format a Message

You have composed an email message in Outlook. Before sending it, you may want to format key parts of the message text. In this topic, you will format the text in an email message.

Some email messages contain important information that may need to be formatted differently from the rest of the message. Outlook provides formatting options that can make a section stand out, draw the recipient's attention, and ensure that it is not lost among the other contents of the message.

The Mini Toolbar

The *Mini* toolbar is a floating toolbar that is displayed beside text that has been selected. It consists of commonly used text formatting options, including font name, size, color, format painter, bold, italics, and text alignment. You can use any of these available commands without having to access the commands from the Ribbon. The Mini toolbar disappears when you move the mouse pointer away from the selected text.

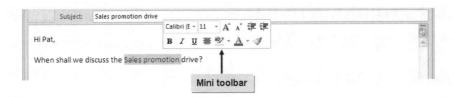

Figure 2-4: The Mini toolbar displaying options that are used to apply font changes to a selected text.

Live Preview

The *Live Preview* feature in Outlook 2010 enables you to preview formatting changes before actually applying the setting to an object. When you place the mouse pointer over an option in a gallery, the effect of the selected option can be previewed in the Message form. Live Preview allows you to experiment with different options before deciding on the one that best suits your needs.

Paste Options

In Outlook 2010, when you copy content or objects and paste them, a contextual hover menu with different paste options is displayed. These paste options can also be accessed by right-clicking anywhere in the body of the email message, or by using the **Paste** drop-down list on the **Home** tab of the Ribbon. These paste options are enabled with the Live Preview functionality, allowing you to preview the appearance of content before pasting it.

There are four paste options that can be used to paste content differently in an email message.

Paste Option	Description
Use Destination Theme	The pasted content retains the style name that is associated with the copied text, but it uses the style definition of the message where the text is being pasted.
Keep Source Formatting	The pasted content is displayed with the same formatting as the source content.
Merge Formatting	The pasted content adapts the formatting of the content in the location in which it is pasted.
Keep Text Only	The pasted content is stripped of all formatting and graphics and is copied as plain text.

How to Format a Message

Procedure Reference: Format a Message

To format a message:

1. Select the text you want to emphasize.
   - Click before the text you want to select, hold down **Shift** and then click at the end of the text.
   - Click at the beginning of the text, hold down the mouse button, and drag to the end of the text.
   - On the **Format Text** tab, in the **Editing** group, from the **Select** drop-down list, select **Select All.**
2. Apply the format.
   a. If necessary, in the Message form, select the **Format** tab.
   b. Apply the desired formatting options.
      - In the **Format** group, select the **HTML, Plain text,** or **Rich text** option.

      > HTML is the Hyper Text Markup Language and messages can be sent in this format. Plain text is the normal text that is used to draft email messages. The rich text format is proprietary to Microsoft e-mailing software, and is compatible with Outlook and Outlook Express.

      - In the **Font** group, set the desired options.
      - In the **Paragraph** group, set the desired options.
      - In the **Styles** group, set the **Style set, Styles,** and **Font** settings.

Procedure Reference: Format Text Using the Mini Toolbar

To format text using the Mini toolbar:
1. Display a Message form.
2. Type text in the message body.
3. Select the text that needs to be formatted.
4. Apply the desired formatting options from the Mini toolbar.
   - From the **Font** drop-down list, select the desired font.
   - From the **Font size** drop-down list, select the desired font size.
   - Select the **Grow font** or **Shrink font** option.
   - Select the **Decrease indent** or **Increase indent** option.
   - Set the **Bold, Italic, Underline,** and **Center** settings.
   - Set the **Font color** and **Text Highlight Color** settings.

ACTIVITY 2-2
Formatting a Message

Scenario:
In the message you are composing to forward a candidate's resume, you want to set the font size and formatting options.

1. Set the font for the message text as Arial.

   a. In the Message form, select the **Format Text** tab, and in the **Editing** group, from the **Select** drop-down list, select **Select All.**

   b. In the **Font** group, from the **Font** drop-down list, select **Arial.**

   c. Click anywhere to deselect the text.

2. Apply bold formatting to the text "tomorrow."

   a. In the message body, click before the word "tomorrow," hold down **Shift,** and click at the end of the sentence to select the word "tomorrow."

   b. On the **Format Text** tab, in the **Font** group, click **Bold.** **B**

3. Change the font size of the message text.

   a. On the **Format Text** tab, in the **Editing** group, from the **Select** drop-down list, select **Select All.**

   b. In the **Font** group, from the **Font Size** drop-down list, select **12.**

   c. Click anywhere in the message body to deselect the text.

4. Change the font and size of the text "3Rz Learning" using the Mini toolbar.

   a. In the message body, click before the text "3Rz Learning," hold down **Shift,** and click at the end of the sentence to select the text "3Rz Learning."

   b. Observe that the Mini toolbar appears above the selected text.

   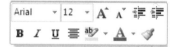

   c. On the Mini toolbar, click the **Bold** button.

d. On the Mini toolbar click the **Font Color** drop-down arrow, and in the **Standard Colors** section, select **Blue,** the eighth color from the left.

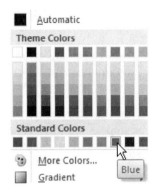

e. Click anywhere in the message body to deselect the text.

TOPIC C
Check Spelling and Grammar

You formatted an email message. It is a good idea to ensure that messages are error free before sending them. In this topic, you will check the spelling and grammar of an email message.

When typing an email message, there is a possibility of introducing spelling or grammatical errors. A message sent with spelling and grammatical errors can appear unprofessional, and can distract from the intent of the message. Using Outlook's spelling and grammar features ensures that there are no spelling or grammatical errors in the message before you send it.

The AutoCorrect Feature

The *AutoCorrect* feature detects common typing mistakes, including misspelled words, grammatical errors, incorrect capitalization, and typographical errors. By default, spelling and grammar are automatically checked when you type a message. Wavy red underlines indicate a possible spelling error and wavy green underlines a possible error in grammar. The auto-suggestion list appears with options to change words, stop auto correcting, or set the AutoCorrect options.

The AutoCorrect Options Button

The **AutoCorrect Options** button is displayed below a letter or word that is modified by using the AutoCorrect feature. This button opens a pop-up menu that provides options to undo automatic corrections, to stop particular automatic corrections, or to modify AutoCorrect options by using the **AutoCorrect** dialog box.

The Spelling and Grammar Dialog Box

Outlook allows you to run a spelling and grammar check in your draft content using the **Spelling and Grammar** dialog box. The dialog box can be launched from the **Proofing** group on the **Review** tab. The dialog box provides various options to correct spelling and grammar errors in email messages.

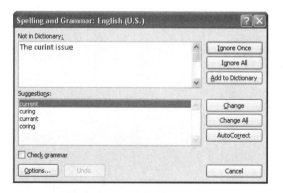

Figure 2-5: *The Spelling and Grammar dialog box displaying options to run a spelling and grammar check on content.*

Option	Description
Not in Dictionary	Lists words that are misspelled or sentences with grammatical errors.
Suggestions	Lists the correct spelling for misspelled words and the correct usage for grammatical errors.
Ignore Once	Allows you to ignore the current occurrence of the misspelled word.
Ignore All	Allows you to ignore all the occurrences of the misspelled word throughout the text.
Add to Dictionary	Allows you to add the words listed in the **Not in Dictionary** list box to the dictionary without changing the way the words have been typed in the text.
Change	Allows you to change the highlighted misspelled words after entering the correct spelling in the text or choosing the correct option from the **Suggestions** list.
Change All	Allows you to change all occurrences of the misspelled word.
AutoCorrect	Allows you to apply the AutoCorrect options.
Options	Allows you to display the **Outlook Options** dialog box and set editorial preferences such as spell check, AutoCorrect, and proofing.
Undo	Allows you to delete the action that was performed last in a sequence of actions.
Cancel	Allows you to cancel the spelling and grammar check that is run on the email message.

The Translation Feature

Outlook allows you to select text in an email message that you received or compose and translate the text it into a language of your choice. You can select text in a message form and send it to an online translation service, translate selected text to a different language using the Research pane, or use the Mini Translator to translate selected text into a different language.

Audio Transcription of Text

The Mini Translator allows you to hear an audio version of text that is selected in a message. Audio transcription is available for all languages supported by Outlook.

How to Check Spelling and Grammar

Procedure Reference: Check the Spelling and Grammar of a Message

To check the spelling and grammar of a message:

1. In the Message form, draft a message that is to be checked for spelling and grammatical errors.
2. On the **Review** tab of the Message form, in the **Proofing** group, click **Spelling & Grammar** to display the **Spelling and Grammar** dialog box.
3. Correct any word that Outlook does not recognize.
   - Click **Ignore Once** to skip the current occurrence of the word.

   The **Spelling and Grammar** dialog box disappears as you make changes with the **Ignore, Change, Change all,** and **Ignore Once** options.

   - Click **Ignore All** to skip all occurrences of the word.
   - Click **Add to Dictionary** to keep the word unchanged and add the word to the user dictionary so it does not get flagged as a misspelled word during later checks.
   - Click **Change** after you change the spelling of the word by either entering a different spelling or selecting a word from the **Suggestions** list box.
   - Click **Change All** to change the spelling of all instances of the word in the message.
4. If necessary, in the **Microsoft Outlook** message box, click **Yes** to continue checking the text of the entire message.
5. Click **OK** to close the **Microsoft Outlook** dialog box.

Procedure Reference: Use the AutoCorrect Feature on Text

To use the AutoCorrect feature on text:

1. Display a Message form.
2. In the Message form, type the text in the message body.
3. If there are errors in the text, AutoCorrect highlights such text. Click below an incorrect word.
4. The **Auto Suggestions** list appears with suggestions on how the word is to be typed.
5. From the **Auto Suggestions** drop-down list, select a suggestion to apply it to the word.
6. If necessary, send the message.

Procedure Reference: Translate Text in a Message Received or in a Composed Message

To translate text in a message received or in a composed message:

1. Display a message
   - Open a received message.
   - Compose a message.
2. Select the desired text.

3. Display the translation options.
   - In the Message form that displays the received message, on the **Message** tab, in the **Editing** group, click the **Translate** button.
   - In the Message form that displays the composed message, on the **Review** tab, in the **Language** group, click the **Translate** button.
4. From the displayed drop-down list select the desired option.
   - Select **Translate Item** to display the **Translate Whole Document** dialog box and select the desired option.
     - Select **Send** to send the item to a machine translation service.
     - Select **Do not send** to prevent the item from being sent to a machine translation service.
   - Select **Translate Selected Text** to display the **Research** pane.
     - In the **Research** pane, in the **Translation** section, from the **From** drop-down list, select the desired language.
     - In the **Research** pane, in the **Translation** section, from the **To** drop-down list, select the desired language.
   - Hover the mouse pointer over a word or phrase, and in the **Mini Translator,** select the desired option.
     - Select **Expand** to display the **Research** pane.
     - Select **Copy** to copy the text.
     - Select **Play** to hear an audio transcription of the selected text.
     - Select **Stop** to stop the audio transcription from being played.
     - Select **Help** to display the **Outlook Help** dialog box.

ACTIVITY 2-3
Checking the Spelling and Grammar

Scenario:
Before you send a message to a coworker, you want to ensure that the message is error free.

1. Check the text for spelling errors.

   a. Place the insertion point at the beginning of the message text.

   b. On the Ribbon, select the **Review** tab.

   c. Select the **Review** tab, and in the **Proofing** group, click **Spelling & Grammar.**

   d. If necessary, in the **Spelling and Grammar : English (U.S)** dialog box, click **Resume.**

   e. In the **Spelling and Grammar : English (U.S)** dialog box, in the **Not in Dictionary** list box, verify that the wrongly spelt word "postion" is highlighted in red.

   f. In the **Suggestions** list box, observe that the first word suggested is **position** and that it is selected.

   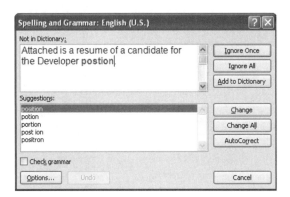

   g. Click **Change** to replace the misspelled word "postion" with the correct word "position."

2. Correct the spacing error.

a. In the **Spelling and Grammar : English (U.S) dialog box,** dialog box, in the **Not in Dictionary** list box, verify that the text "workingfor" is highlighted in red.

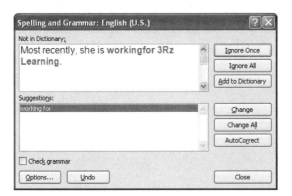

b. In the **Suggestions** list box, observe that the suggested replacement is the text **working for.**

c. Click **Change** to replace the text with correct spacing between the words.

d. In the **Microsoft Outlook** message box, which indicates that the spelling check is complete, click **OK.**

3. Check the functionality of the AutoCorrect feature.

   a. In the message body, click in the blank line above the text "Regards" and press **Enter.**

   b. Type *tihs* to start the next paragraph.

   c. Press the **Spacebar.**

   d. Observe that the typed word is automatically corrected to "This" with the correct casing and spelling.

   e. Move the mouse pointer over the word "This" and place the mouse pointer over the blue line to display the **AutoCorrect Options** drop-down arrow.

   f. Click the drop-down arrow to display the AutoCorrect options.

   g. In the **AutoCorrect Options** drop-down list, observe that the AutoCorrect settings are listed.

   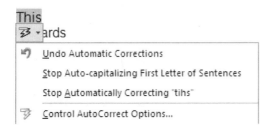

h. Click immediately after the word "This" to close the **AutoCorrect Options** drop-down list.

i. In the message body, type *is an excellent resume.* Press **Enter**.

TOPIC D
Attach a File

You checked the spelling and grammar of an email message. When sending email messages, you may often need to send additional information that cannot be composed as part of the message. In this topic, you will attach a file to an email message.

You may have information in a file that you wanted to share. Retyping the information would be an unnecessary and time-consuming exercise. The information may also be in the form of an image, video, or audio file that you cannot add to the body of the email message. The email feature in Outlook allows you to send files and other attachments with your email message.

Attachments

Definition:
An *attachment* is a file that you have access to that is sent along with an email. Attachments are denoted with an icon representing the specific file type. The attached file is commonly displayed with its file name, type, and size.

Example:

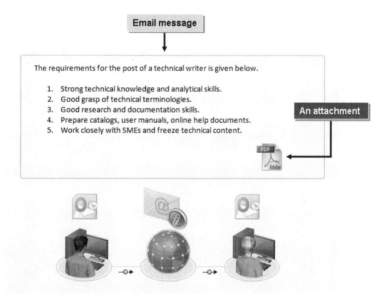

Figure 2-6: An attachment that is sent with an email.

File Type and Size Guidelines
There are a few file type and size guidelines that you should follow when attaching files to an email.
- Make sure that the recipient of an attachment will be able to open and read the attachment. The recipient must have the application with which the attachment was created, or an application in which the file type is compatible.
- Be aware of the attachment size because very large attachments require a lot of space and consume more time while sending and receiving the message.

- The attachment size can be limited by the mail server. An attachment larger than the limit results in a failure to send, or a failure to be received by the recipient's mail server size limits.

How to Attach a File

Procedure Reference: Attach a File to an Email Message

To attach a file to an email message:

1. Open a new Message form.
2. Type the recipient's name, the subject, and the message body.
3. In the Message form, select the **Message** tab.
4. In the **Include** group, click **Attach File.**
5. In the **Insert File** dialog box, navigate to the desired file or folder.
6. Attach a file.
   - Double-click the file you want to attach or;
   - Select the file you want to attach and click **Insert.**

ACTIVITY 2-4
Attaching a File

Data Files:

C:\084595Data\Composing Messages\Resume.docx

Scenario:

You need to send the candidate's resume with the email that you have composed. The resume is a large document and you cannot spend time retyping the data from the resume in your message. You decide to send the resume as an email attachment.

1. Attach a file to the message.

    a. Select the **Message** tab, and in the **Include** group, click **Attach File**.

    b. In the **Insert File** dialog box, navigate to the C:\084595Data\Composing Messages folder.

    c. Double-click **Resume.docx.**

    d. Observe that in the Message form below the **Subject** text box, an **Attached** text box is added and the file icon, name, and size of the attached file are displayed.

    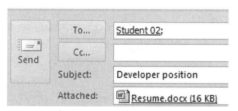

2. Which information will be displayed for an attached file?
    a) File name
    b) File type
    c) File size
    d) File creation date

TOPIC E
Enhance an Email Message

You attached a file to an email message. You may also want to insert objects such as tables, images, and charts in an email message and modify their appearance. In this topic, you will enhance an email message.

Often email messages include additional information such as tables, images, and charts, which help convey the intended meaning more effectively. These objects may not be added to every email message, and any options to work with these objects need to appear only when such objects are included in a message. In Outlook, tabs containing these options are displayed only when the object is selected so that you can modify the appearance and properties of the object.

Contextual Tabs

Contextual tabs are tabs that appear on the Ribbon only when you select specific objects such as charts, tables, drawings, or text boxes in a message. The commands and options available on these tabs are restricted to those that can be used to manipulate the specific type of object included in the active email message. Contextual tabs are displayed in addition to the existing command tabs on the Ribbon.

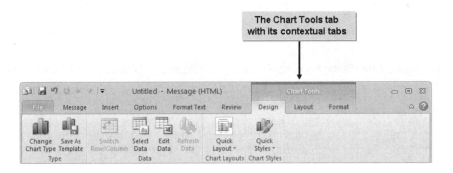

Figure 2-7: *The contextual tabs displayed in addition to the existing command tabs.*

Types of Contextual Tabs

Outlook provides three types of contextual tabs: **Format, Design,** and **Layout.** One or more of these contextual tabs appear when an object is selected or inserted within an email message. Depending on the object selected, the contextual tab options may differ.

Contextual Tab	Appears When You
Format	Insert or select pictures, text boxes, shapes, charts, WordArt, SmartArt graphics, and clip art within an email message. The commands within this tab can be used to format a selected object. You can change the object style, modify its color, or change its position in the email message.

Contextual Tab	Appears When You
Design	Insert or select tables, charts, equations, and SmartArt graphics within an email message. The commands within this tab can be used to make design changes, such as the style in which the object is presented within the email message.
Layout	Insert or select tables, charts, pictures, and shapes, or draw text boxes within an email message. The commands within this tab can be used to change the layout of an existing chart or modify a table by merging, splitting, or inserting rows. Using this tab, you can also modify the alignment of text within the objects.

Tool Tabs

Tool tabs are tabs that contain any of the Format, Design, or Layout contextual tabs, or a combination of them. The **Tool** tabs are enabled when you work on an object in an email message. The following are some of the commonly used Tool tabs that are displayed while working with an email message.

Tool Tab	Displays
Table Tools	The **Design** and **Layout** contextual tabs on the Ribbon. The commands within these tabs can be used to apply a table style, modify an existing style, add colors, and create borders. In addition, you can change the layout of a table by merging cells, inserting and deleting rows and columns, changing cell sizes and alignment, and converting data in a table to plain text.
Picture Tools	The **Format** contextual tab on the Ribbon. The commands on this tab can be used to modify the appearance of images by increasing or decreasing the brightness and contrast, apply a picture style by making a selection from a gallery, or apply effects. You can remove the unwanted portions of an image and compress them to reduce the size of the messages. You can also provide images with an outline and arrange them in coordination with other images.
Drawing Tools	The **Format** contextual tab on the Ribbon. The commands on this tab can be used to specify the direction of text in a text box; apply a text box style, shadow, and 3D effects; and specify the size and position of text boxes in an email message. It can also be used to include shapes; apply colors, effects, and styles to shapes; apply shadow and 3D effects; and position shapes in a message. Additionally, you can edit WordArt, increase or decrease the spacing between words, apply styles and effects, and position WordArt objects in an email message.
Chart Tools	All three contextual tabs on the Ribbon. The **Design** tab can be used to change the chart type and save a newly created template, if any. You can also pick an existing chart style and layout in addition to editing the source data. The **Layout** tab can be used to include pictures and shapes, if needed. You can also add chart elements such as titles, labels, gridlines, and axes. The **Format** tab can be used to change the fill and outline color of objects and text, select WordArt styles, reduce or increase chart sizes, and arrange charts in messages along with the text.

Tool Tab	Displays
SmartArt Tools	The **Format** contextual tab on the Ribbon. The commands on this tab can be used to enhance the presentation of information in the form of graphics, tables, and charts.
ClipArt	The **Format** contextual tab on the Ribbon. The commands on this tab can be used to increase or decrease the brightness, contrast, and color of the images. You can apply a style or position the clip art and ensure that text wraps around it. Unwanted portions of the clip art can also be cropped.
Ink Tools	The **Pens** contextual tab on the Ribbon. The commands on this tab can be used to compose messages in a specific color and thickness.
Equation Tools	The **Design** contextual tab on the Ribbon. The commands on this tab can be used to insert symbols and equations in an email message.

Galleries

A *gallery* is a library that lists a set of predefined styles that can be applied to objects, such as text, graphics, tables, and shapes, when composing a message. Most of the commands on the Ribbon have galleries, which provide you with gallery options. Some galleries are also accessible from shortcut menus, giving you quick access to gallery options.

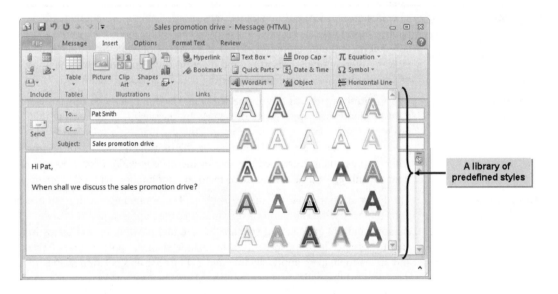

Figure 2-8: Predefined styles displayed in the gallery.

Themes

A *theme* is a set of design and formatting choices that are applied to a message to ensure overall consistency. A theme specifies the fonts and colors to be used for text, and the effects for shapes, charts, and diagrams that are inserted in the message. There are several predefined themes on the **Options** tab of the Ribbon. You can either pick an existing theme for your message or create a theme by customizing an existing theme. The newly created theme can also be applied to other messages.

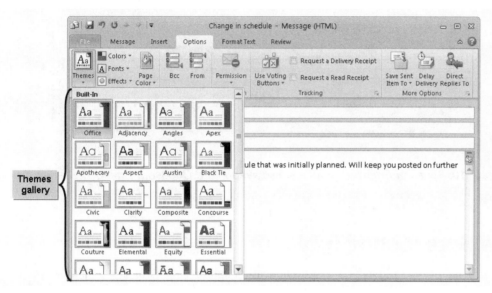

Figure 2-9: The Themes gallery displaying design and formatting choices that can be applied to a message.

Styles

A *style* is a set of formatting options, such as fonts, colors, and paragraph spacing, which can be applied to text that is typed in the Message form. You can apply a style, change the style, have a preferred style set, and also set a style as the default with the existing style options in Outlook.

SmartArt

SmartArt is a visual representation of a formatted layout that can be added to Outlook mail messages. A SmartArt graphic allows you to convey information in a format that can be easily understood and recalled by the receiver of email messages. A SmartArt graphic layout is editable, allowing you to display your information in a pre-set diagram as a helpful aid to your message recipients. The **Choose a SmartArt Graphic** dialog box provides options to add SmartArt in the form of a **List, Process, Cycle, Hierarchy, Relationship, Matrix, Pyramid,** and **Picture.** These layouts can be used as they are, or you can incorporate your own design and formatting changes using the available contextual tab commands.

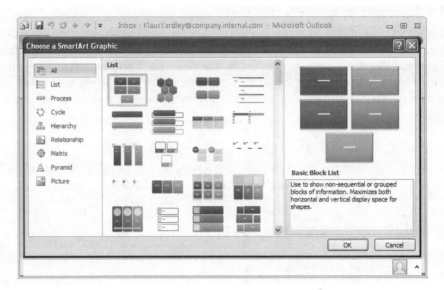

Figure 2-10: Types of SmartArt graphics displayed in the Choose a SmartArt Graphic dialog box.

The Screenshot Tool

The **Screenshot** tool allows you to automatically capture screens of any available window, or manually capture only a portion of a window or screen. This tool is available on the **Illustrations** group of the **Insert** tab. The captured screenshot is automatically inserted in an email message. You can then use the various image editing options that are available on the contextual tabs within the **Picture Tools** tool tab to modify the screenshot, as required.

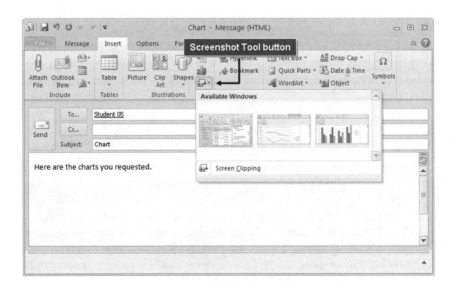

Figure 2-11: The Screenshot tool is used to capture the screenshot of an open window.

The Background Removal Tool

The *Background Removal* tool allows you to separate an object from its background by removing the background of the image while retaining the object. The **Remove Background** command is available in the **Adjust** group of the **Format** contextual tab of the **Picture Tools** tool tab. When you use this command, the background area of the image is highlighted in purple. You can then use the tools in the **Background Removal** contextual tab to mark the areas that need to be retained, and those that need to be removed.

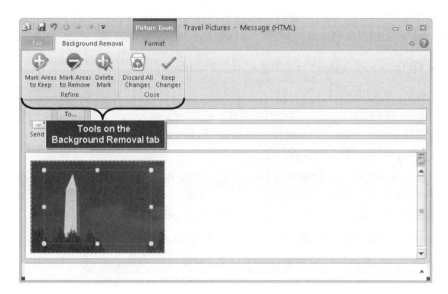

Figure 2-12: *The Background Removal tool marks the areas to be removed or retained.*

How to Use the Contextual Tab Commands

Procedure Reference: Set a Default Font for Messages

To set a default font for messages:

1. Open a Message form.
2. In the Message form, select the **Format Text** tab.
3. In the **Styles** group, from the **Change Styles** drop-down list, select **Fonts** and then select the desired font.
4. From the **Change Styles** drop-down list, select **Set As Default** to set the selected font as the default font.

Procedure Reference: Apply a Theme to a Message

To apply a theme to a message:

1. Display a Message form.
2. In the message body, type the desired text.
3. On the Ribbon, select the **Options** tab.

4. In the **Themes** group, specify the desired settings.
   - Click the **Themes** drop-down arrow and select a theme to be applied to the message.
   - If necessary, click the **Colors** drop-down arrow and select a color to be applied to the message.
   - If necessary, click the **Font** drop-down arrow and select a font to be applied to the message.
   - If necessary, click the **Effects** drop-down arrow and select an effect to be applied to the message.
5. If necessary, send the message after drafting the complete text.

Procedure Reference: Insert a Shape in a Message

To insert a shape in a message:

1. In the message body, type the desired text.
2. Place the insertion point anywhere you need to insert a shape.
3. On the Ribbon, select the **Insert** tab.
4. On the **Insert** tab, in the **Illustrations** group, click the **Shapes** drop-down arrow and from the gallery, select a shape.
5. Click and drag in the Message form to add the shape.
6. Click anywhere in the message body to deselect the shape.

Procedure Reference: Insert a SmartArt Graphic in a Message

To insert a SmartArt graphic in a message:

1. In the message body, type the desired text.
2. Place the insertion point where you want to insert a SmartArt graphic.
3. On the Ribbon, select the **Insert** tab.
4. On the **Insert** tab, in the **Illustrations** group, click **SmartArt** to display the **Choose a SmartArt Graphic** dialog box.
5. In the **Choose a SmartArt Graphic** dialog box, select a SmartArt graphic and click **OK**.
6. Click anywhere in the message body to deselect the SmartArt graphic.

Procedure Reference: Insert a Picture in a Message

To insert a picture in a message:

1. In the message body, place the insertion point in the desired location.
2. On the Ribbon, select the **Insert** tab.
3. In the **Illustrations** group, click **Picture** to display the **Insert Picture** dialog box.
4. In the **Insert Picture** dialog box, navigate to the folder with the image that you want to insert.
   - Select the image and click **OK** or;
   - Double-click the image.

Procedure Reference: Compress an Inserted Picture

To compress an inserted picture:

1. If necessary, in an email, insert a picture.
2. Select the picture.

3. Compress the picture to reduce the file size.
   a. On the **Picture Tools** tool tab, on the **Format** contextual tab, in the **Adjust** group, click **Compress Picture.**
   b. If necessary, in the **Compress Picture** dialog box, set the compression settings.
      - Check the **Apply only to this picture** check box to apply the compression settings to the selected picture alone.
      - Check the **Delete cropped areas of pictures** check box to delete the cropped areas of the picture, which are not visible.
      - Select the **Print** option to compress the picture so that it is of a high quality suitable for printing.
      - Select the **Screen** option to compress the picture for best output when used on a web page or displayed using a projector.
      - Select the **E-mail** option to minimize the size for sharing through email.
   c. Click **OK** to close the **Compression Settings** dialog box.

Procedure Reference: Capture Screenshots

To capture screenshots:
1. Place the insertion point at the desired location in the email message.
2. Select the **Insert** tab, and in the **Illustrations** group, click **Screenshot.**
3. In the displayed gallery, select an option to capture the screenshot.
   - Select the window that you want to capture a screenshot of.
   - Select **Screen Clipping** to capture a region of the window.
4. If necessary, click and drag to mark the area of the window that you need to capture.
5. The screenshot is inserted in the email message. If necessary, in the message body, drag the image placeholder to reposition the image.

Procedure Reference: Edit an Image

To edit an image:
1. Select the image that needs to be edited. The **Picture Tools** tool tab is displayed on the Ribbon.
2. Select the **Format** contextual tab.
3. If necessary, use the options provided in the **Adjust** group to modify the image.
   - Adjust the color, brightness, and contrast of the image.
   - Add artistic effects to the image.
   - Remove the background of the image.
     a. Click **Remove Background.**
     b. Use the options on the **Background Removal** contextual tab to define the areas on the image to keep or remove.
     c. On the **Background Removal** contextual tab, from the **Close** group, choose a command to save or discard the changes to the image.
4. In the **Picture Styles** group, specify the settings to apply the desired style, effect, and border to the image.
5. In the **Arrange** group, specify the settings to set the position of the image.

6. In the **Size** group, specify the settings to resize the image.
7. Click outside the image to view the results.

Microsoft® Office Outlook® 2010: Level 1

ACTIVITY 2-5
Enhance an Email Message

Data Files:

C:\084595Data\Composing Messages\Logo.jpg

Scenario:

Now that you have completed drafting a message, run a spell check, and formatted the message, you want to enhance the appeal of the message. You also want to add your company logo below your signature. Because the logo image is around 25 KB, you decide to compress the file before you send the email.

1. Change the page color of the message.

    a. Select the **Options** tab, and in the **Themes** group, click the **Page Color** drop-down arrow, and then in the displayed gallery, in the **Theme Colors** section, select the **Orange, Accent 6 Lighter 80%** color, which is the last color in the second row of the section.

    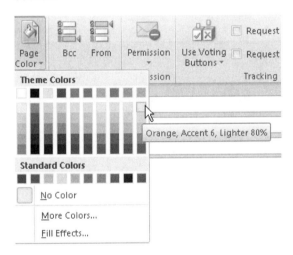

    b. Observe that the page color of the message is changed.

2. Insert a picture file.

    a. In the message body, click at the end of the word "Regards" and press **Enter**.

    b. Select the **Insert** tab, and in the **Illustrations** group, click **Picture**.

Lesson 2: Composing Messages

c. In the **Insert Picture** dialog box, navigate to the C:\084595Data\Composing Messages folder.

d. Select **Logo.jpg** and click **Insert.**

3. Compress the picture file.

   a. On the **Picture Tools** tool tab, on the **Format** contextual tab, in the **Adjust** group, click the **Compress Pictures** button.

   b. In the **Compress Pictures** dialog box, in the **Compression options** section, verify that the **Apply only to this picture** check box is checked and click **OK.**

ACTIVITY 2-6
Using SmartArt, Themes, and Styles in Email Messages

Before You Begin:
Minimize the Developer Position message.

Scenario:
Your manager wants you to send an email explaining the hierarchy chart of employees in your office so that he can include the hierarchy details when he makes a presentation. You want to send the chart by email and enhance it so that it looks presentable.

1. Draft the hierarchy email message.

    a. On the **Home** tab, in the **New** group, click **New E-mail** to open a new Message form.

    b. In the Untitled Message - (HTML) window, in the **To** text box, type *student00* and press **Tab** twice.

    c. In the **Cc** text box, type your partner's user name and press **Tab** twice.

    d. In the **Subject** text box, type *Employee hierarchy* and press **Tab.**

    e. In the message body, type *Hello* and press **Enter** twice.

    f. Type *Here is the employee hierarchy information that you needed.* Press **Enter** twice.

2. Add a SmartArt graphic to the message.

    a. Select the **Insert** tab, and in the **Illustrations** group, click **SmartArt** to display the **Choose a SmartArt Graphic** dialog box.

    b. In the **Choose a SmartArt Graphic** dialog box, in the left pane, click **Hierarchy.**

    c. In the middle pane, select the **Hierarchy** SmartArt graphic, which is the first graphic in the second row and click **OK.**

    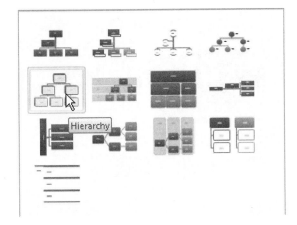

    d. Observe that the SmartArt graphic is inserted into the message body.

e. In the **Type your text here** pane, click the **Close** button.

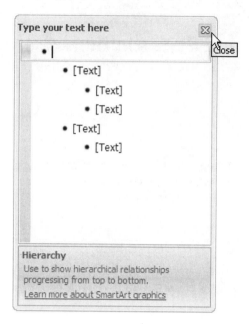

3. Enter the manager and senior executive details in the Hierarchy SmartArt graphic.

   a. At the top of the SmartArt graphic that is inserted in the message body, in the first text box, click and type *Manager* and press **Enter.**

   b. Type *P. Smith*

   c. Below the text box that contains the text "Manager", in the text box placed on the left, click and type *Senior HR Executive 1* and press **Enter.**

   d. Type *A. Jackson*

   e. Below the text box that contains the text "Manager", in the text box placed on the right, click and type *Senior HR Executive 2* and press **Enter.**

   f. Type *M. Muller*

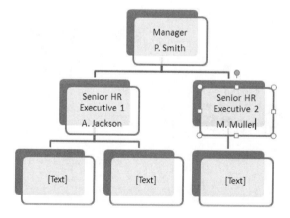

4. Enter the details of junior executives.

a. Below the text box that contains the text Senior HR Executive 1, in the first text box from the left, click and type *Junior HR Executive 1* and press **Enter.**

b. Type *R. Moore*

c. In the second text box from the left, click and type *Junior HR Executive 2* and press **Enter.**

d. Type *J. Rivera*

e. In the third text box from the left, click and type *Junior HR Executive 3* and press **Enter.**

f. Type *J. Dillon*

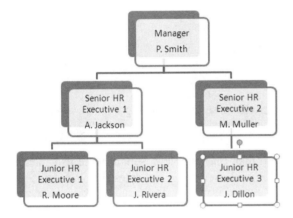

g. To the right side of the SmartArt graphic, click immediately outside the graphic to deselect it and press **Enter** twice.

h. Type *Regards*

5. Apply a theme and style to the message.

   a. On the Ribbon, select the **Options** tab and in **Themes** group, from the **Themes** drop-down list, select **Equity.**

   b. Observe that the SmartArt graphic in the message body appears different now.

   c. Select the **Format Text** tab, and in the **Styles** group, from the **Change Styles** drop-down list, select **Fonts** and then select **Office Classic 2** to change the font style of the SmartArt graphic.

TOPIC F
Send an Email Message

You composed an email message using various Outlook features. You may now want to ensure that the message reaches its intended recipients. In this topic, you will send an email message.

A large amount of professional correspondence is delivered through email communication. This involves sending email messages to different recipients. By using an email application such as Outlook, you can communicate to multiple recipients using various options.

How to Send a Message

Procedure Reference: Send a Message

To send a message:

1. Compose a message.
2. To the left of the **To** text box, click **Send** to send the message.

Address messages

If you are addressing the message to more than one recipient, separate the user names with a semicolon (;). In the **To** text box, an underlined user name indicates that it matches a name on the global address list.

Procedure Reference: Resend a Message

To resend a message:

1. In the Navigation pane, in the **Mail Folder** section, select the Sent Items folder.
2. In the View pane, double-click the message that needs to be resent.
3. On the **Message** tab of the Message form, in the **Move** group, from the **More Move Actions** drop-down list, select **Resend This Message.**
4. If necessary, in the **To** text box, type a different email address to resend the message to a different recipient.
5. In the Message form, click **Send** and close the original Message form.

Save Messages

While composing a message, you might feel that the message is short of necessary information and that it cannot be sent. You can save the message by choosing **Save** on the **File** tab and send it later. The message gets stored in the Drafts folder. When you are ready to finish the message, you can open the message, add the desired information to the Message form, and send it.

Procedure Reference: Recall or Resend a Message

To recall or resend a message:

1. Display the contents of the Sent Items folder.
2. Open the message you want to recall or resend.

3. If necessary, recall a message.
   1. Select the **File** tab and click the **Resend or Recall** button.
   2. From the displayed drop-down list, select **Recall This Message.**
   3. In the **Recall This Message** dialog box, select the desired option.
      - Select **Delete unread copies of this message** to delete the copy of your email in the recipients inbox.
      - Select **Delete unread copies and replace with a new message** to delete the copy of your email from the recipients inbox and replace it with a new message.
4. If necessary, resend a message.
   - Select the **File** tab and click the **Resend or Recall** button.
   - From the displayed drop-down list, select **Resend This Message.**
5. Click **OK** and close the message form.
6. In the Navigation pane, in the Sent Items folder, verify whether the message you replaced is displayed.

ACTIVITY 2-7
Sending and Resending a Message

Before You Begin:
The Employee Hierarchy message window is displayed.

Scenario:
You have drafted an email detailing that a candidate be considered for the Developer position. You have run a spell check and done all formatting for it to be in a perfect shape. Now, you need to send the email to the intended recipient. In addition, you also want to send the employee hierarchy message that you drafted to the manager.

1. Send the composed messages.

    a. In the Employee hierarchy - Message (HTML) window, click **Send** to send the message to Student00 and a copy to your partner.

    b. Restore the Developer position - Message (HTML) window.

    c. Click **Send** to send the email with the attachment.

2. Resend the message to another recipient.

    a. In the Navigation pane, in the **student##@company.internal.com** section, select the Sent Items folder.

    b. In the View pane, double-click the **Developer position** message to open it.

    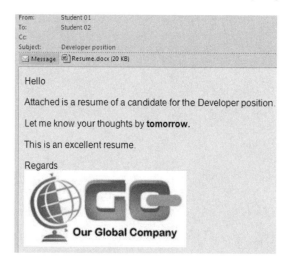

    c. On the **Message** tab, in the **Move** group, from the **Actions** drop-down list, select **Resend This Message.**

    d. Observe that a new Message form with the Developer position message is opened.

    e. In the Message form that is displayed, in the **To** text box, click on your partner's name to select it and press **Delete.**

f. In the **To** text box, type ***student00*** and press **Tab.**
g. Click **Send.**
h. Click the **Close** button to close the Developer position - Message (HTML) window.

Lesson 2 Follow-up

In this lesson, you composed email messages. Composing email messages with proper formatting and ensuring that they are error free will help you convey the intended meaning accurately.

1. **What Outlook email features do you use the most often while composing messages?**

2. **Which features would you prefer to use to enhance the appearance of your mail messages?**

3 | Organizing Messages

Lesson Time: 35 minutes

Lesson Objectives:

In this lesson, you will organize email messages into folders.

You will:

- Manage email messages.
- Move email messages into different folders.
- Open and save an attachment.

Introduction

You sent and received email messages. As the number of messages in your Inbox increases, you may want to manage the messages effectively to access them easily. In this lesson, you will organize messages.

You may receive many messages and, as a result, your Inbox may end up cluttered. You may face a situation when it is critical to find an important message you need at short notice. By organizing your email messages, you can keep them easily accessible and retrieve the email that you need without needing to panic.

TOPIC A
Manage Email Messages

You deleted email messages in Outlook. You may want to mark other messages using indicators so that they can be retrieved easily when needed. In this topic, you will use the mail management features in Outlook to mark and prioritize messages.

You often provide an email address while registering with a site, or unintentionally sign up for newsletters. This results in receiving a lot of messages in which neither you are interested nor you find any use. Outlook 2010 makes it easy to identify the messages that you want to read and to ignore the unwanted ones by marking them. There may also be email messages that you want to keep track of and respond to later.

Message Flagging

Outlook enables you to *flag* a message with an icon to indicate whether the message needs a follow-up action. You may want to refer to the flagged message for important information or forward its content at a later date. A message can be flagged for follow-up by setting a default option or using the **Custom** option to add a customized date and time. The **Add Reminder** option allows you to set a reminder for following up the flagged message. When a message is flagged, not only will it appear in the View pane with the follow-up flag, but it will also be placed on the **To-Do** bar. In addition, all messages that are flagged are automatically placed in the For Follow up folder. You can remove a flag by selecting the **Clear Flag** option.

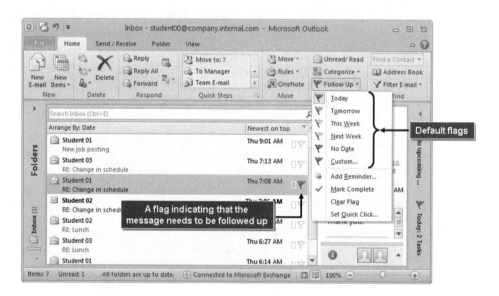

Figure 3-1: The flag options are displayed in the drop-down list.

Flag Types
You can apply different types of flags to messages.

Flag Type	Description
Today	Sets the flag to a selected time in the current day.
Tomorrow	Sets the flag for the next day.
This Week	Sets the flag to the last day of the current week.
Next Week	Sets the flag to the last day of the next week.
No Date	Sets the flag with no date mentioned.
Custom	Sets the flag to a desired date specified in the **Custom** dialog box.
Add Reminder	Sets the flag to a desired date with a reminder. It is indicated by a bell symbol.

The Ignore Command

The **Ignore** command in Outlook provides options to move messages that are part of a conversation to the Deleted Items folder. If a conversation thread is selected to be ignored, then the current and the future email messages that are part of the conversation are ignored. You can also recover conversations that were ignored from the Deleted Items folder.

The Clean Up Command

The **Clean Up** command, available in the **Delete** group of the **Home** tab, helps you move all old, redundant messages to the folders you choose. By default, messages that are cleaned up are sent to the Deleted Items folder. You can also move the cleaned-up messages into a folder you create. As this command helps you move messages out of the Inbox, you can ensure that space is available in the Inbox for additional messages that are received. The unwanted messages are moved and the recent messages are displayed in the View pane. The **Clean Up** command helps delete messages, subfolders, and folders. The options to clean up a specified set of messages and folders, and the location to which the cleaned-up items will be moved can be set in the **Outlook Options** dialog box.

MailTips

The *MailTips* feature in Outlook 2010 provides real-time feedback on messages before they are sent. To enable the display of MailTips, you need to configure Outlook with a Microsoft Exchange 2010 server and the MailTips need to be defined on the server. As you compose a message, Outlook and Exchange work together to determine if any MailTips apply to your message and then display them above the address fields.

Commonly Used MailTips

There are different MailTips that are displayed for different issues that come up when composing an email message. They also suggest actions that can be taken for an issue to be corrected. Additionally, MailTips can also be displayed for meeting and task requests. Multiple MailTips can be displayed for an email message.

MailTip	Description
Restricted Recipient	Displayed when you lack the permission to send an email message to a specific recipient. If the message is sent, it will be returned as undelivered.
Moderated contact group	Displayed when a contact group has a moderator. The moderator moderates the incoming email messages to determine whether or not the message should be delivered to the contact group.
Invalid recipient address	Displayed when the recipient's address is invalid.
Message too large for recipient	Displayed when the size of the outgoing message exceeds the size limit specified for incoming messages by one or more of the recipients.
Message too large to send	Displayed when the size of the outgoing message exceeds the specified outgoing message size.
Mailbox quota about to be exceeded	Displayed when the message being composed will push your mailbox quota over the limit, so that it will not be possible to send more messages until the mailbox is freed.

How to Manage Mail Messages

Procedure Reference: Flag a Message for Follow Up

To flag a message for follow up:

1. Select the message to be flagged.
2. Flag the message.
   - In the View pane, right-click the message to be flagged, choose **Follow Up** and choose a flag type or;
   - Open the message to be flagged, and on the **Message** tab, in the **Tags** group, click the **Follow Up** drop-down arrow and select a flag type or;
   - On the **Home** tab, in the **Tags** group, click **Follow Up** and then select a flag type.
3. If necessary, view the flagged message in the For Follow Up folder.
   a. On the **Folder** tab, in the **New** group, click **New Search Folder.**
   b. In the **New Search Folder** dialog box, in the **Select a Search Folder** section, select the **Mail flagged for Follow Up** option and click **OK.**
   c. In the Navigation pane, click the For Follow Up folder to view the flagged messages.
4. If necessary, from the **Follow Up** drop-down list, remove a flag by selecting the desired option.
   - Select **Clear Flag** to remove the flag.
   - Select **Mark Complete** to mark the message as complete.

Procedure Reference: Flag a Message for Follow Up with a Reminder

To flag a message for follow up with a reminder:

1. Select the message to be flagged.

2. In the **Follow Up** drop-down list, select the desired options to add a flag with a reminder.
   - Select the **Custom** option to add a flag for the desired custom date.
   - Select the **Add Reminder** option to add a flag for the desired custom date with a reminder.

 The reminder is set by default when the **Add Reminder** option is selected. The reminder needs to be set when the **Custom** option is selected.

3. In the **Custom** dialog box, set the flagging options as desired.
   - From the **Flag to** drop-down list, select the desired option.
   - Click the **Start date** drop-down arrow to select a start date from the displayed calendar.
   - Click the **Due date** drop-down arrow to select a due date from the displayed calendar.
   - Check the **Reminder** check box if the flagged message needs a reminder, and from the Reminder date drop-down list, select the desired date and from the Reminder time drop-down list select the desired time.
4. Click **OK** to close the **Custom** dialog box.
5. If necessary, in the Navigation pane, click the **Search Folder** list to view the For Follow Up folder with the flagged messages.

Set a Quick Click Option

The **Set Quick Click** option in the **Follow Up** drop-down list allows you to add or remove a flag with just a click. This option allows you to mark a **Quick Flag** for a selected item. For example, from the **Follow Up** drop-down list, if you select **Tomorrow** and then set the **Set Quick Click** option, when clicking any of the messages, the **Tomorrow** option will be applied. By default, the **Set Quick Click** option is set for **Today.**

Procedure Reference: Mark a Message as Unread

To mark a message as unread.
1. In the Inbox, either select or open the message that you want to mark as unread.
2. Mark the message as unread.
   - Select the **Home** tab, and in the **Tags** group, click **Read/Unread** or;
   - Right-click the message and choose **Mark as Unread.**

Procedure Reference: Clean Up Messages

To clean up messages:
1. Select a conversation or folder from which you want to clean up messages.
2. On the **Home** tab, in the **Delete** section, click the **Clean Up** drop-down arrow.

3. From the drop-down list, select the desired option.
   - Select **Clean Up Conversation** to clean up the selected conversation and move messages from the selected conversation to the Deleted Items folder.
   - Select **Clean Up Folder** to clean up the selected folder and move messages from the selected folder to the Deleted Items folder.
   - Select **Clean Up Folder & Subfolders** to clean up the selected folders and subfolders and move messages from them to the Deleted Items folder.

Procedure Reference: Specify Clean Up Settings

To specify clean up settings:

1. On the **File** tab, choose **Options** to display the **Outlook Options** dialog box.
2. In the **Outlook Options** dialog box, in the left pane, click **Mail** to display the **Conversation Clean Up** section.
3. In the **Conversation Clean up** section, specify the desired clean up settings.
   - To the right of the **Cleaned up items will go to this folder** text box, click the **Browse** button and specify a folder where the cleaned up items will be stored.
   - In the **Messages moved by Clean up will go to their account's Deleted items** section, select the desired options.
4. Click **OK** to close the **Outlook Options** dialog box.

Procedure Reference: Ignore a Conversation

To ignore a conversation:

1. In the Inbox, select a conversation that you want to ignore.
2. On the **Home** tab, in the **Delete** group, click **Ignore.**

 You can also open the message, and in the **Delete** group of the **Message** tab, click the **Ignore** button.

3. In the **Ignore Conversation** dialog box, click **Ignore Conversation.**

ACTIVITY 3-1
Flagging a Message

Scenario:
Samantha Alvarez has requested you for some information on her job prospects that she had discussed with you earlier. She has sent you an email seeking clarifications. You look into the email and decide to follow up with Samantha so that you can arrange to process her resume further by flagging the message. Then you realize that you will not be able to send her a reply the next day and want to take it up only on the day after tomorrow. So, you remove the flag set to be followed up on the next day.

1. Flag the Request for information message with a reminder to follow up on it the next day.

   a. In the Navigation pane, in the **student##@company.internal.com** section, select Inbox.

   b. In the View pane, scroll down and select the **Request for Information** message.

   c. On the **Home** tab, in the **Tags** group, from the **Follow-Up** drop-down list, select **Tomorrow**.

   d. In the View pane, at the right end of the message, verify that a flag symbol in pale red color is displayed indicating that the message needs to be followed up the next day.

   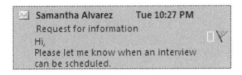

2. Display the For Follow Up folder.

   a. On the Ribbon, select the **Folder** tab, and in the **New** group, click **New Search Folder.**

   b. In the **New Search Folder** dialog box, in the **Select a Search Folder** list box, in the **Reading Mail** section, select the **Mail flagged for follow up** option and click **OK**.

c. Observe that in the Navigation pane, in the **student##@company.internal.com** section, the For Follow-Up(1) folder is selected and in the View pane the "Request for Information" message is displayed.

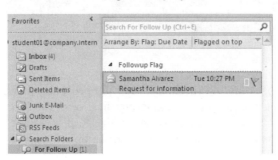

3. Remove the flag from the message.

   a. In the Navigation pane, in the **student##@company.internal.com** section, select the **Inbox**.

   b. In the View pane, right-click the **Request for Information** message and choose **Follow Up→Clear Flag**.

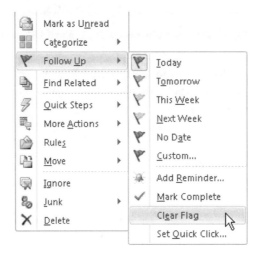

ACTIVITY 3-2
Ignoring a Conversation

Scenario:
A conversation that is old and redundant to current times is not required to be displayed in the View pane whenever you open Outlook. You want to ignore it. You also want to check whether the email messages, received as part of the conversation you selected to ignore, are sent directly to the Deleted Items folder. In addition, you want to specify a location for storing the cleaned-up messages when you perform a clean up of redundant messages.

1. Ignore the Change in schedule message.

    a. In the View pane, scroll down and select the **Change in schedule** message.

    b. On the **Home** tab, in the **Delete** group, click **Ignore.**

    c. In the **Ignore Conversation** message box, click **Ignore Conversation.**

    d. Observe that the Change in schedule message is not displayed in the View pane.

2. Check whether the reply received for the Change in schedule message is displayed in the Deleted Items folder.

    a. In the Navigation pane, in the **student##@company.internal.com** section, select the **Deleted Items** folder.

    b. Observe that in the Deleted Items folder, the reply to the Change in schedule message is displayed.

TOPIC B
Move Email Messages into Folders

You flagged messages in Outlook. It will be easier to find messages if they are organized into different categories. In this topic, you will move email messages into different folders.

You may have many messages in your Inbox that pertain to a variety of topics and that belong to different categories. It may take time for you to locate the messages you need if your Inbox is not organized. You can locate messages quickly if you organize them into specific folders just as you will file your papers. Outlook provides features that help you categorize messages to make tracking and retrieving email messages simpler and quicker.

Default Email Folders

Default email folders are folders that are available in the Outlook application when you launch it. They are used to store email messages. Inbox, Drafts, Sent Items, and Deleted Items, are folders available by default.

Email Folders on the Server

You can create folders in Outlook to organize your mail. These folders are saved in the Exchange server and use storage space in your email Inbox. The size permitted for email allocation is determined by the system administrator.

Personal Folders

Personal folders are folders created in Outlook. Email messages can be moved to these folders. Messages you move to personal folders will be available to you whether you are connected to the network or not. Outlook stores these personal folders as an archive in the hard drive of the system you are using. These archives are saved with the .pst extension.

How to Move Email Messages into Folders

Procedure Reference: Create a Folder

To create a folder:

1. Display the **Create New Folder** dialog box.
   - In the Navigation pane, right-click the desired root folder and choose **New Folder** or;
   - On the Ribbon, on the **Folder** tab, in the **New** group, click the **New Folder** button.
2. In the **Create New Folder** dialog box, in the **Name** text box, specify a name for the folder and click **OK.**

Procedure Reference: Create a Personal Folder

To create a personal folder:

1. Select the **Home** tab, and from the **New Items** drop down list, select **More Items** and then select **Outlook Data File.**
2. In the **Create or Open Outlook Data File** dialog box, navigate to the desired folder and in the **File Name** text box, enter a name of the folder.
3. If necessary, add a password to access the folder.
   a. In the **Create or Open Outlook Data File** dialog box, check the **Add Optional Password** check box and click **OK.**
   b. In the **Create Outlook Data File** dialog box, in the **Password** text box, type a password.
   c. In the **Verify Password** text box, retype the password.
   d. If necessary, check the **Save this password in your password list** check box to save the password.
4. If necessary, in the **Create or Open Outlook Data File** dialog box, click **OK.**

Procedure Reference: Move Messages to Folders

To move messages to a folder:

1. Select the messages that you want to move.
2. Move messages to folders.
   a. Right-click the selected messages, choose **Move** and then choose a folder.
   b. Move the messages to a default email folder.
      A. Right-click the selected messages and choose **Move→Other Folder.**
      B. In the **Move Items** dialog box, select a folder and click **OK.**
3. If necessary, in the Navigation pane, select the folder to which you moved the messages, to confirm that your messages are moved.

Procedure Reference: Copy a Message to a Folder

To copy a message to a folder:

1. Save a copy of a message in a folder.
   - Save a copy using the **Copy to Folder** option.
     a. Navigate to a desired folder.
     b. Select the message that you want to copy.

c. On the Ribbon, on the **Home** tab, in the **Move** group, click the **Move** drop-down arrow and choose **Copy to Folder.**

d. In the **Copy Items** dialog box, select a folder and click **OK.**

- Save a copy using the **Copy** option.

    a. Select the message that you want to copy.

    b. Right-click a selected message and choose **Copy.**

    c. In the Navigation pane, select a folder to which you want to copy the message.

    d. Paste the message in the desired folder.

    - Choose **Copy Folder.**
    - Press **Ctrl+V** to paste the message in the desired folder.

2. If necessary, open the selected folder and verify that the messages are copied to the folder.

Procedure Reference: Move a Folder

To move a folder:

1. In the Navigation pane, select a folder to be moved.
2. Right-click the folder and choose **Move Folder.**
3. In the **Move Folder** dialog box, select a destination folder and click **OK.**
4. If necessary, in the Navigation pane, select the folder to which you have moved the folder and view it.

You can also move folders by dragging them into the desired location.

Procedure Reference: Delete a Folder

To delete a folder:

1. In the Navigation pane, select the folder that you want to delete.
2. Right-click the folder and choose **Delete Folder.**
3. In the **Microsoft Outlook** message box, click **Yes** to confirm the deletion of the selected folder.
4. If necessary, expand the Deleted Items folder to view the deleted folder.

ACTIVITY 3-3
Creating a Folder

Scenario:
Your Inbox is getting full. You want to save some of the messages for future reference. You decide to organize the messages so that your Inbox is not so cluttered and is easier to manage. You feel that you can categorize the messages so that you can store related messages together.

1. Create a folder named Resume in your Inbox.

    a. In the Navigation pane, select the **Inbox.**

    b. On the Ribbon, select the **Folder** tab and in the **New** group, click **New Folder.**

    c. In the **Create New Folder** dialog box, in the **Name** text box, type *Resume*

    d. In the **Select where to place the folder** list box, verify that **Inbox** is selected and click **OK.**

    e. Verify that in the Navigation pane, in the **student##@company.internal.com** section, the Resume folder is displayed as a subfolder of the Inbox.

2. Create two folders named Benefits and Training in the Inbox.

    a. On the **Folder** tab, in the **New** group, click **New Folder.**

    b. In the **Name** text box, type *Benefits*

    c. In the **Select where to place the folder** list box, verify that **Inbox** is selected and click **OK.**

Lesson 3: Organizing Messages 87

d. Similarly, create a folder named *Training* as a subfolder of the Inbox.

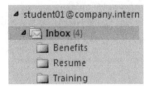

3. Move the Resume of Nancy message to the Resume folder.

   a. In the View pane, scroll up and select the **Resume of Nancy** message.

   b. Right-click the **Resume of Nancy** message and choose **Move→Resume** to move the message to the Resume folder.

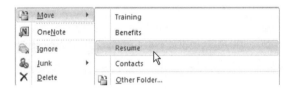

   c. Observe that the Resume of Nancy message is moved from the Inbox.

4. Display the content of the Resume folder.

   a. In the Navigation pane, in the **student##@company.internal.com** section, select the **Resume** folder.

   b. Verify that the Resume of Nancy message is displayed in the View pane as a message in the Resume folder.

5. Move the System training message to the Training folder.

   a. Display the messages in the Inbox.

   b. In the View pane, if necessary, scroll down and select the **System Training** message.

   c. Select the **Home** tab, and in the **Move** group, from the **Move** drop-down list, select **Training.**

   d. Click the Training folder to display its contents in the View pane.

   e. Verify that the System training message is displayed in the View pane.

6. Copy the System training message to the Benefits folder.

   a. On the **Home** tab, in the **Move** group, from the **Move** drop-down list, select **Copy to Folder.**

   b. In the **Copy Items** dialog box, in the **Copy the selected items to the folder** list box, select the **Benefits** folder and click **OK.**

   c. In the Navigation pane, in the **student##@company.internal.com** section, select the **Benefits** folder.

d. Observe that the System Training message is displayed in the View pane indicating that it is copied to the Benefits folder.

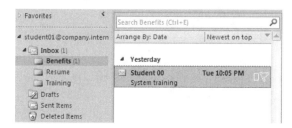

e. Select the **Inbox.**

ACTIVITY 3-4
Moving Folders

Before You Begin:
1. Create a folder named *Tasks* in the Inbox.
2. Select the Tasks folder.

Scenario:
You have created folders in the Inbox. You realize that some folders can be grouped within another folder. As the Training folder contains task-oriented messages, you plan to move the Training folder inside the Tasks folder.

1. Move the Training folder to the Tasks folder.

   a. In the Navigation pane, in the Inbox, right-click the Training folder and choose **Move Folder.**

   b. In the **Move Folder** dialog box, in the **Move the selected folder to the folder** list box, select **Tasks** and click **OK.**

2. Expand the Tasks folder.

   a. In the Navigation pane, in the **student##@company.internal.com** section, to the left of the Tasks folder, click the white triangle, to expand the folder.

   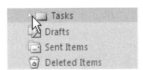

   b. Verify that the Training folder is displayed as a subfolder of the Tasks folder.

   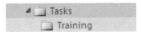

   c. To the left of the Tasks folder, click the black triangle, to close the expanded Tasks folder.

TOPIC C
Open and Save an Attachment

You moved email messages into folders to keep them organized. When you receive an email message with an attachment, you will need to know how to open and save the attached file so that you can access it later. In this topic, you will open and save an attachment.

You received an email message with an attachment. You have read the message, but do not have the time to look through the contents of the attachment. By saving the attachment, you can view it at a more convenient time. Saving an attachment also allows you to delete the email message that you no longer need, thus freeing up space in your Inbox.

Attachment Preview

The *attachment preview* feature allows you to preview a file that is attached to an email message. You can preview the content on the Reading pane even before opening it. This feature allows you to view the attachment without needing to open the attachment in its respective application.

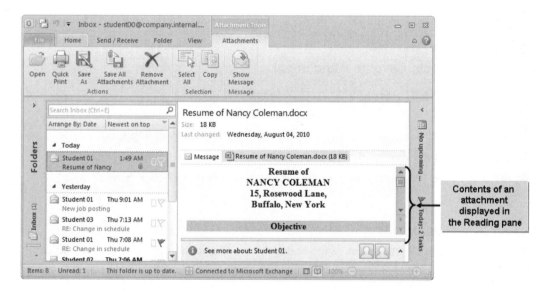

Figure 3-2: A preview of an attachment in the Reading pane.

How to Open and Save an Attachment

Procedure Reference: Preview an Attached File

To preview an attached file:

1. In the Navigation pane, click a folder in which a message is stored with an attachment.
2. Preview the attachment.
    a. In the View pane, select the message with an attachment.
    b. In the Reading pane, click the attachment.
    c. Below the attachment, click **Preview File** to preview the attachment file in the Reading pane.

Procedure Reference: Open an Attachment

To open an attachment:

1. Open a message that contains an attachment.
2. Open the attachment.
    - In the Message form, double-click the attachment to open it.
    - Right-click the attachment and choose **Open.**
3. The attachment opens in the full screen view and after reading through it, if necessary, click **Close** to close the attachment.

Procedure Reference: Save an Attachment

To save an attachment:

1. If necessary, open a message that contains an attachment.
2. Select the **File** tab and choose **Save As** to display the **Save As** dialog box.
3. If necessary, in the **Save As** dialog box, navigate to a desired folder.
4. In the **File name** text box, type a name for the attachment and click **Save.**
5. Close the message.

Delete an Attachment

To delete an attachment, open the message that contains the attachment you want to delete. Below the **Subject** text box, select the attachment and on the **Attachments** tab, in the **Actions** group, click **Remove Attachment.**

ACTIVITY 3-5
Opening and Saving an Attachment

Scenario:

You want to check on one particular resume that you found impressive when you ran through the email. You want to preview the attached resume and save it so that you can look at it after some time to decide on whether the person is suitable for the opening you have in mind.

1. Preview the attachment file.

    a. In the Navigation pane, select the Resume folder.

    b. In the View pane, verify that the Resume of Nancy message is selected.

    c. In the Reading pane, click the **Resume of Nancy Coleman.docx [19 KB]** attachment.

    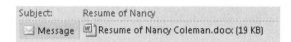

    d. In the Reading pane, observe that a warning message is displayed.

    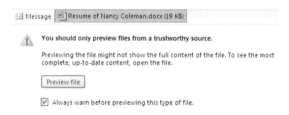

    e. Below the warning message, click **Preview file.**

    f. Verify that the Resume of Nancy Coleman file is displayed in the Reading pane.

    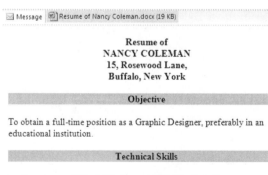

2. Open the file attached to the Resume of Nancy message.

   a. In the Reading pane, double-click the **Resume of Nancy Coleman.docx (19 KB)** attachment.

   b. Verify that the Resume of Nancy Coleman.docx file opens in the Microsoft Word 2010 application.

   c. If necessary, scroll down and read through the resume.

   d. In the Resume of Nancy Coleman.docx (Read-Only) - Microsoft Word window, click the **Close** button to close the document.

3. Save a copy of the attachment.

   a. On the **Attachment Tools** tool tab, on the **Attachments** contextual tab, in the **Actions** group, click **Save As**.

   b. In the **Save Attachment** dialog box, navigate to the C:\084595Data\Organizing Messages folder, and click **Save**.

Lesson 3 Follow-up

In this lesson, you organized your messages. This allows you to easily locate messages and retrieve them easily when you have a large number of email messages to handle.

1. **Why would you prefer to flag certain messages?**

2. **Suggest some folder names under which you will organize your messages.**

4 Managing Contacts

Lesson Time: 1 hour(s)

Lesson Objectives:

In this lesson, you will manage contacts and contact information.

You will:

- Add a contact to the Outlook Address Book.
- Sort and find contacts.
- Find the geographical location of a contact by generating a map.
- Update contact information.

Introduction

You organized your email messages in Outlook. If you communicate with certain people frequently, you can save their email addresses, along with other details so that you do not have to remember or retrieve them from other places. In this lesson, you will manage contacts in Outlook.

You have a huge collection of business cards that are organized, but the email address or fax number you are looking for in a hurry always seems to be the hardest to find. Outlook 2010 makes it easy to store and organize all contact information of your business and personal associates. Details of contacts such as email addresses, phone and fax numbers can be easily searched, retrieved, and updated.

TOPIC A
Add a Contact

You opened and saved attachments received from people you communicate with. If you interact with these people on a frequent basis, you may want to store their email addresses and retrieve them for use whenever you need. In this topic, you will add a contact.

In the course of your workday, you may have frequent interactions with many people and they may provide you with their email addresses, contact numbers, and fax numbers that you may need to communicate with them. At times, you may also need the email address of a key client, and you may not have that person's email address readily available. This means that each time you need to send a message, you have to search for and type the email address. There may even be occasions when you misspell an email address, resulting in the email message not being delivered. Storing important contact information in Outlook allows you to retrieve it when needed.

Contacts

A *contact* is a person with whom you communicate on a business or personal level, and whose personal or business information or both need to be stored and retrieved. When you enter the name of a contact, Outlook records the name in the **File as** field. You can sort, group, and filter contacts by any part of the name or address you want. It is the name of the contact that you will enter in the **To** text box in the Outlook Message form, when you draft email messages.

The Contact Form

The *Contact form* is used to enter information related to contacts in Outlook. This form contains fields and text boxes in which you can enter personal and business information relating to contacts such as name, company, job title, email addresses, and phone numbers. Adding a contact to the Outlook Contact folder helps you retrieve chosen contacts for use whenever you draft email messages to them. Contact information can be updated as and when needed. You can create a contact using the **New Contact** button in the **New** group on the **Home** tab.

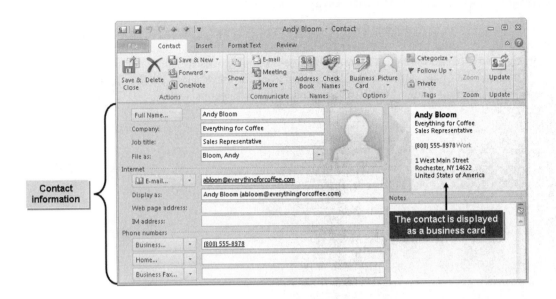

Figure 4-1: Fields of the Contact form.

The Contact Form Fields
The Contact form allows you to enter data in various fields.

Fields	Allows You To
Full Name	Enter the full name of a contact.
Company	Enter the company name of a contact.
Job title	Enter the job title of a contact.
File as	Select from suggestions on category names under which the contact information will be filled in the contacts list.
Email	Enter the email address of a contact.
Display as	Enter a name for the contact which can be displayed instead of the email address.
Web page address	Enter the URL of a contact's website.
IM address	Enter the Instant Messenger ID of a contact.
Phone Numbers	Enter the business, home, business fax, and mobile phone numbers of a contact.
Notes	Enter any additional information pertaining to a contact.
Addresses	Enter the residence and the office address.

Electronic Business Cards

An *electronic business card* is a feature that is used to share contact information through email. The electronic business card is designed to appear like a printed business card. It displays the name of the contact, the company the contact works for, the designation, phone numbers, and the email address. Contact information in these cards can be displayed with company logos, different backgrounds, photos, and other images as well.

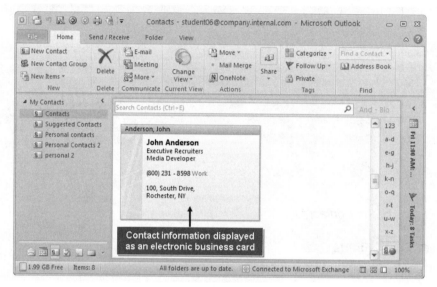

Figure 4-2: Electronic business cards can be sent through email.

Contact Views

Outlook provides a variety of options to display contact information so that you can view information in your preferred style. You can view contacts in the form of **Business Card, Card, Phone,** or **List.** The default view is the Business Card view. You can change these views using the **Change View** button in the **Current View** group on the **View** tab of the Contact form. You can set the current view as a new view and also apply a chosen view to other contact folders.

Color Categories

Outlook allows you to categorize items and assign color codes to each category. Assigning color categories to messages, contacts, appointments, and tasks enables you to quickly identify or track them and associate them with other related items. You can also customize a category's color and name. The **Categorize** button in the **Tags** group on the **Home** tab helps you assign color categories to items.

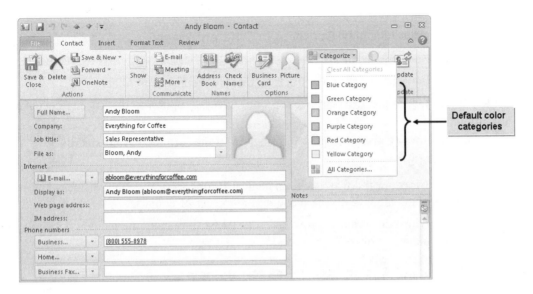

Figure 4-3: The Categorize drop-down list displaying the color categories.

Secondary Address Books

A *secondary address book* is an additional address book you can create in Outlook to store contact details. By default, contacts are stored in the default address book that is created during installation. Contact information from other applications such as Excel can be imported and stored in the secondary address book. You can create more than one secondary address book depending upon how you want contact information to be organized.

How to Add a Contact

Procedure Reference: Add a Contact

To add a contact to the Outlook Address Book:

1. On the Quick Launch bar, click **Contacts** to display the content of the Contacts folder.
2. On the Ribbon, in the **New** group, click **New Contact** to display a new Contact form.
3. In the new Contact form, enter the desired information in the appropriate text boxes.
   - In the **Full name** text box, enter the name of the contact.
   - In the **Company** text box, enter the details of the company.
   - In the **Job title** text box, enter a title.
   - From the **File as** drop-down list, select an option.
   - In the **Internet** section, enter the necessary details.
   - In the **Phone numbers** section, enter the necessary details.
   - In the **Addresses** section, enter the necessary details.
4. If necessary, enter additional information about contacts.
   a. On the **Contact** tab, in the **Show** group, click **Details** to enter additional information in the Details form.
   b. In the Details form, enter the necessary information.
5. On the **Home** tab, in the **Actions** group, click **Save & Close**.

6. In the Contact form, on the **Contact** tab, in the **Actions** group, click **Save & Close.**

Procedure Reference: Display Contacts in Different Views

To display contacts in different views:

1. On the Quick Launch bar, click **Contacts** to display the Contacts folder.
2. On the **Home** tab, in the **Current View** group, select an option to display the contacts in a desired view.
   - Click **Business Card** to display information in the form of business cards.
   - Click **Card** to display the contacts as cards.
   - Click the **More** drop-down arrow and select **Phone** to display the business and home phone numbers along with the name and company of contacts.
   - Click the **More** drop-down arrow and select **List** to display the name, company, job title, and phone numbers of contacts.

Procedure Reference: Assign Categories to Contacts

To assign categories to contacts:

1. Select a contact to which you want to assign a category.
2. Assign a category to a contact.
   - Assign an existing category to a contact.
     a. On the **Contact** tab, in the **Tags** group, from the **Categorize** drop-down list, select **All Categories.**
     b. In the **Color Categories** dialog box, select a color category.
     c. If necessary, in the **Rename Category** dialog box, in the **Name** text box, type a name and click **Yes** to rename the category.
   - Assign a new category to a contact.
     a. On the **Contact** tab, in the **Tags** group, from the **Categorize** drop-down list, select **All Categories.**
     b. In the **Color Categories** dialog box, click **New.**
     c. In the **Add New Category** dialog box, in the **Name** text box, type a name.
     d. If necessary, from the **Color** and **Shortcut Key** drop-down lists, select a color and a shortcut key, respectively.
     e. Click **OK** to display the new category in the **Color Categories** dialog box.
     f. In the **Color Categories** dialog box, click **OK.**

Procedure Reference: Create a Contact from Another Contact

To create a contact from another contact:

1. Display the Contacts folder.
2. Double-click a contact based on which information you will create another contact.
3. In the Contact form, on the Contact tab, in the **Actions** group, click the **Save** drop-down arrow and select **Contact from the Same Company.** A new Contact form is displayed for you to fill in the required details.
4. If necessary, fill in the required details, save, and close the form.

Procedure Reference: Create a Contact from the Message Header

To create a contact from the message header:

1. Display an email message.
2. Double-click the message, and in the open message, right-click the name of the sender and choose **Add to Outlook Contacts** to display a new Contact form.
3. If necessary, add details about the contact.
4. Save and close the Contact form.

Procedure Reference: Create a Secondary Address Book

To create a secondary address book:

1. On the Ribbon, select the **Folder** tab, and in the **New** group, click **New Folder.**
2. In the **Create New Folder** dialog box, in the **Name** text box, type a name for the address book.
3. From the **Folder Contains** drop-down list, select **Contacts Items.**
4. In the **Select where to place the folder** list box, select a folder and click **OK**.

Procedure Reference: Import Contacts Stored in an Excel File into a Secondary Address Book

To import contacts stored in an Excel file into a secondary address book:

1. On the Quick Launch bar, click **Contacts** to open the Contacts folder.
2. In the Navigation pane, click a secondary address book that you created.
3. Select the **File** tab and choose **Open**, and in the Backstage view, click **Import**.
4. In the **Import and Export Wizard,** in the **Choose an action to perform** list box, verify that the **Import from another program or file** option is selected and click **Next**.
5. On the **Import from a File** page, in the **Select a file type to import from** section, select **Microsoft Excel 97–2003** and click **Next**.
6. To the right of the **File to import** text box, click the **Browse** button to display the **Browse** dialog box.
7. In the **Browse** dialog box, navigate to a desired location, select an Excel file, and click **OK**.
8. On the **Import a file** page, click **OK** to display the **Import a file** dialog box.
9. In the **Import a file** dialog box, click **Next**.
10. In the **Select a destination folder** section, select the folder where you want the contacts from the Excel file to be stored and click **Next**.
11. On the **Import a file** page, click **Finish**.

Format of Contacts Stored in an Excel Sheet

Contacts saved in an Excel sheet can be imported into the Contacts folder and the secondary address book only if the fields in the Excel sheet are mapped to the correct Outlook format. This mapped format of the Excel sheet can be created by exporting the contacts from the Contacts folder into the Excel sheet. Then, the format of this sheet can be used to add contacts and import them into an Excel sheet. Mapping of these fields can also be done by using the **Map Custom Fields** button in the **Import a File** dialog box.

ACTIVITY 4-1
Adding a Contact

Scenario:

Now that you are communicating with your clients and candidates for various jobs, you have obtained a lot of personal information. You want to store this information in one place, so that when you need to contact someone, you can quickly access it. You have just met a client, Margaret Sherwood, with whom you will have extensive communication through email and telephone. You want to store her contact information for future reference.

1. Display a new Contact form.

    a. On the Quick Launch bar, click **Contacts**.

    b. On the Ribbon, on the **Home** tab, in the **New** group, click **New Contact** to display a Contact form.

    c. Maximize the Contact form.

2. Add the contact details for Margaret Sherwood.

    a. In the **Full Name** text box, type *Margaret Sherwood* and press **Tab**.

    b. Observe that the **File as** text box is filled with the last name and the first name.

    c. In the **Company** text box, type *Citizens Info* and press **Tab**.

    d. In the **Job title** text box, type *Senior Executive*

    e. In the **Internet** section, in the **E-mail** text box, click and type *msherwood@citizensinfo.org* and then press **Tab**.

    f. Observe that the **Display as** text box is filled with the email address and name.

    g. In the **Phone numbers** section, in the **Business** text box, click and type *716–555–4444* and press **Tab**.

    h. In the **Location Information** dialog box, in the **What area code (or city code) are you in now** text box, click and type *14622* and then click **OK**.

    i. In the **Phone and Modem Options** dialog box, click **OK**.

j. In the **Home** text box, type *585–555–4445*

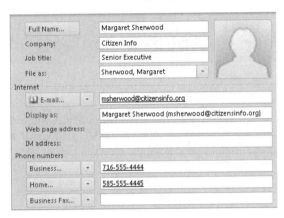

3. Add Margaret's business and home addresses.

   a. In the **Addresses** section, in the **Business** text box, click and type *Highland Parkway, Suite 301* and press **Enter**.

   b. Type *Buffalo, NY 14204* and press **Enter**.

   c. In the **Addresses** section, click the **Business** drop-down arrow and select **Home**.

   d. In the **Home** text box, type *222 Cullens Drive* and press **Enter**.

   e. Type *Rochester, NY 14622*

4. Assign this contact to the **Business** category.

   a. On the **Contact** tab, in the **Tags** group, from the **Categorize** drop-down list, select **Blue Category**.

   b. In the **Rename Category** dialog box, in the **Name** text box, type *Business* and click **Yes** to rename and assign the category.

   c. Observe that a blue color bar, with the text **Business** is displayed at the top of the Contact form.

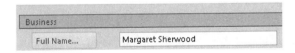

   d. In the Contact form, on the **Contact** tab, in the **Actions** group, click **Save & Close**.

ACTIVITY 4-2
Creating a Contact Based on Another Contact

Scenario:
You want to add the contact details of John Anderson to the existing contacts. Incidentally, you find out that the details of the contact you want to include are the same as those of the already existing contact, Mina Hajay, except for the name and designation.

1. Create a contact from another contact.

    a. In the View pane, scroll down and double-click the business card of Mina Hajay to display a Contact form with the contact information.

    b. In the Contact form, on the **Contact** tab, in the **Actions** group, from the **Save & New** drop-down list, select **Contact from the Same Company.**

    c. Verify that a new Contact form is displayed with the same company information as that of Mina Hajay.

2. Fill in the complete contact information for John Anderson.

    a. In the **Full Name** text box, type *John Anderson*

    b. In the **Job title** text box, click and type *Junior Executive*

    c. On the **Contact** tab, in the **Actions** group, click **Save & Close.**

    d. Close the Contact form that displays the details for Mina Hajay.

ACTIVITY 4-3
Creating a Contact from a Message Header

Scenario:
You have received an email from the human resources manager of a company asking you to send resumes related to graphic designer and media developer positions. Because you will be dealing with the HR manager in the future, you decide to save the information about the HR manager as a new contact with the basic input available from the message header.

1. Create a contact from a message header.

    a. On the Quick Launch bar, click **Mail,** and in the Navigation pane, select the **Inbox.**

    b. In the View pane, double-click the Registration information message.

    c. In the Registration Information - Message (HTML) window, right-click **Susan Yong** and choose **Add to Outlook Contacts.**

2. Add contact details.

    a. In the Contact form, in the **Company** text box, click and type *Ristell & Sons Publishing*

    b. In the **Job title** text box, click and type *HR Manager*

    c. In the Contact form, on the **Contact** tab, in the **Actions** group, click **Save & Close.**

    d. Close the Registration information - Message (HTML) window.

    e. On the Quick Launch bar, click **Contacts** to display the contacts.

    f. In the View pane, scroll down to view the contacts.

g. Observe that the Contact form of Susan Yong is displayed in the Contacts folder.

ACTIVITY 4-4
Creating a Secondary Address Book and Importing Contacts from Excel

Data Files:
C:\084595Data\Managing Contacts\Personal contacts.xls

Scenario:
You have all your official contacts stored in the Contacts folder of the Outlook Address Book. Now, you wish to create a secondary address book to store all your personal contacts. You have all the contact information of your friends in an Excel sheet. Instead of copying each contact separately, you decide to import the Excel sheet as a whole into your new secondary address book.

1. Create a secondary address book.

    a. On the Ribbon, select the **Folder** tab, and in the **New** group, click **New Folder.**

    b. In the **Create New Folder** dialog box, in the **Name** text box, type *Personal Contacts*

    c. In the **Folder contains** drop-down list, verify that **Contact Items** is selected.

    d. In the **Select where to place the folder** list box, verify that **Contacts** is selected and click **OK.**

e. In the Navigation pane, in the **My Contacts** section, select the Personal Contacts folder.

2. Import the contacts in the Excel worksheet to the **Personal Contacts** address book.

   a. On the Ribbon, select the **File** tab and choose **Open**.

   b. In the Backstage view, click **Import**.

   c. Observe that in the **Import and Export Wizard,** in the **Choose an action to perform** list box, the **Import from another program or file** option is selected and click **Next**.

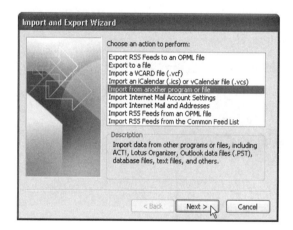

   d. On the **Import a file** page, in the **Select a file type to import from** list box, select **Microsoft Excel 97-2003** and click **Next**.

   e. In the **File to import** section, click **Browse**.

   f. In the **Browse** dialog box, navigate to the C:\084595Data\Managing Contacts folder.

   g. Select the **Personal Contacts.xls** file and click **OK**.

   h. On the **Import a File** page, click **Next**.

i. In the **Select destination folder** section, click **Next** to accept the Personal Contacts folder as the destination folder for the new contacts.

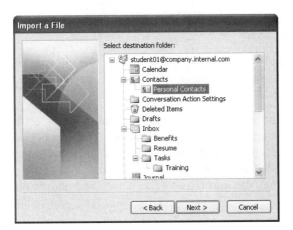

j. Click **Finish** to import the contacts.

3. Check whether the import from Excel was successful.

    a. Observe that the contacts are displayed in the Personal Contacts folder.

    b. In the Navigation pane, select the Contacts folder.

TOPIC B
Sort and Find Contacts

You added contacts to your Outlook Address Book. To quickly locate the contact information in your address book, you have different options available in Outlook. In this topic, you will sort and find contacts.

When you have a large number of contacts, it is very difficult to quickly find specific contacts. It will be easier to find contacts in an address book if they are sequenced in a defined order. Also, when you need to print the contacts, it is useful to have them in an alphabetical order so that you can quickly locate the contact that you want on the printed list. You can also group your contacts by their organization so that you can retrieve the names and addresses of all the contacts in an organization.

Sort Orders

A *sort order* is the sequence in which items are arranged. Sorting the contacts based on specific criteria allows you to arrange the contacts in a defined sequence so that you can easily locate your contacts. You can sort contacts by criteria such as full name, company, phone numbers, or email addresses. The **Reverse sort** button allows you to reverse the order in which contacts are sorted in a click. This button is available in the **Arrangement** group on the **View** tab.

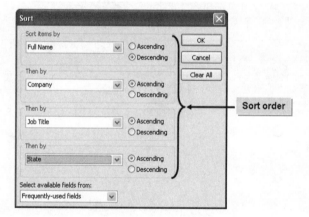

Figure 4-4: Sort order conditions specified in the Sort dialog box.

The Find Group

The **Find** group in Outlook allows you to find contacts in an address book and filter contacts as well. The **Find a Contact** text box in the **Find** group on the **Home** tab allows you to find contacts. When you type the name of a contact in this text box, Outlook displays the Contact form for that particular contact so that you can quickly read through the information related to that contact.

How to Sort and Find Contacts

Procedure Reference: Sort Contacts

To sort contacts:

1. Display the Contacts folder.
2. On the Ribbon, select the **View** tab.
3. On the **View** tab, in the **Current View** group, click **View Settings.**
4. In the **Advanced View Settings** dialog box, click **Sort.**
5. In the **Sort** dialog box, select the desired order to sort the contacts.
   - In the **Sort items by** section, from the drop-down list, select a sort field.
   - Select either the **Descending** or **Ascending** option to sort contacts based on the ascending or descending order of the selected field.
   - From the first **Then by** drop-down list, select a sort field and set the ascending or descending sort option.
   - If necessary, from the other **Then by** drop-down lists, select an option and set the ascending or descending sort option to add more sort criteria.
   - If necessary, from the **Select available fields from** drop-down list, select an option to sort contacts by this field.
6. Click **OK** to sort the contacts.

Sorting Contacts Based on Column Header

You can sort contacts by columns such as name, company, business phone, business fax, home phone, mobile phone and email address. You can click a column header to sort the contacts based on the information stored in that column. when contacts are sorted based on a column a small triangle appears to the right of the column name indicating that the list of contacts has been sorted based on that column. An upward pointing arrow indicates that the contacts are sorted in ascending order, and a downward pointing arrow indicates that contacts are sorted in descending order.

Procedure Reference: Find a Contact

To find a contact:

1. On the **Home** tab, in the **Find** group, click in the **Find a Contact** text box to activate it.
2. Type the name, company name, or other text, which you want to use as your search keyword.

 If you have searched for this contact previously, you can click the **Find a Contact** drop-down arrow and choose a search term from the list.

3. Press **Enter** to display any contact that contains information that matches the word or words you entered.
4. If necessary, close the Contact forms.

Searchable Terms

When you enter a word or phrase in the **Find a Contact** text box, Outlook looks in the Contacts folder for a word or phrase that matches the word entered. By default, Outlook only searches for partial names, first or last names, email addresses, display as names, and company names.

ACTIVITY 4-5
Sorting and Finding Contacts

Scenario:
You are sending invitations for an upcoming seminar on recruitment policies in your company. You want to send invitations to all your contacts at Rudison Technologies because you have sent a lot of candidates to the company for hiring. Because the contacts are scattered throughout the list, you have to go through multiple pages of contact names to determine the ones you need. It will be easier if you can display all the Rudison Technologies contacts together on one page in various views. You also want to sort the contacts in Rudison Technologies using their job titles so that you get a view of all the titles in the contacts that need to be invited.

1. Sort the list by name in alphabetical order.

    a. In the Navigation pane, in the **My Contacts** section, verify that the Contacts folder is selected.

    b. Select the **Home** tab, and in the **Current View** group, click the **More** button and select **Phone.**

    c. In the View pane, click the **Full Name** column header to sort the list of contacts in alphabetical order by full name.

2. Search for contacts working with Rudison Technologies.

    a. In the View pane, in the **Search Contacts** text box, click and type *Rudison* and then press **Enter.**

    b. Observe that a list of contacts working with Rudison Technologies is displayed.

    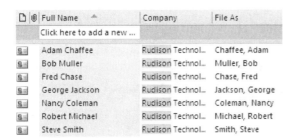

    c. On the **Home** tab, in the **Current View** group, click the **More** button and select **Business Card** to view the contact details as business cards.

    d. On the Ribbon, on the **Search Tools** tool tab, select the **Search** contextual tab, and in the **Close** group, click **Close Search.**

TOPIC C
Find the Geographical Location of a Contact

You sorted the contacts in your address book. You may sometimes need to travel to meet a contact for a personal interaction. In this topic, you will generate a map of the geographical location of a contact.

When you have a meeting scheduled with a client at the client's location, you may have the address, but may not know how to get there. By using Outlook, you can quickly refer to a map, so that you can find your way there without worrying about being late for the meeting.

The Map It Option

The *Map It* option helps you locate the address of a contact in a visual format. It is available in the **More** drop-down list in the **Communicate** group of the **Contact** tab. It generates a map for the location of a contact based on the address entered for the contact. The map has options to zoom in or out of it, print it, and get directions to a location. It is essential that the complete address of contacts is entered in Outlook for the **Map It** option to be used.

How to Find the Geographical Location of a Contact

Procedure Reference: Generate a Map

To generate a map:

1. Display the Contact form of a contact.
2. Display a map of the location of the contact in Internet Explorer.
   - On the **Contact** tab, in the **Communicate** group, from the **More** drop-down list, select the **Map It** option or;
   - In the Contact form, in the **Addresses** section, click **Map It.**
3. If necessary, in Internet Explorer, double-click the address on the map to zoom in to the address on the map. Click again to zoom out.
4. In Internet Explorer, click the **Close** button and close the Contact form.

ACTIVITY 4-6
Generating a Map

Scenario:
The sales manager of a client has a plan to recruit sales personnel and he has spoken to you in this regard. You have arranged for a personal meeting with him so that you can discuss the hiring details. You need to travel to the location mentioned in his Contact form in Outlook. You are not sure how to get there and want to use a map to reach the location.

1. Display a map to John Smith's business address.

     Students should ensure that their computers are connected to the Internet before starting the activity.

    a. In the Contacts folder, scroll down and double-click the business card for **John Smith** to display a Contact form with information pertaining to John Smith.

    b. In the Contact form, in the **Addresses** section, click **Map It.**

2. Zoom in to view the location on the map.

    a. Maximize the Internet Explorer window.

    b. Observe that in the Internet Explorer window, the address is marked on the map with an orange filled circle.

    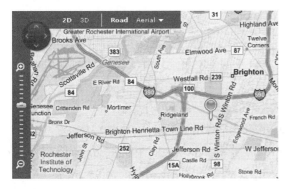

    c. Double-click the orange filled circle to zoom in on the address.

    d. In the Internet Explorer window, click the **Close** button.

    e. Close the Contact form.

TOPIC D
Update Contacts

You have searched for the geographical location of a contact. When there is a change in addresses, phone numbers, or other information you have stored for a contact, you may need to keep your address book updated. In this topic, you will update contact information in your Outlook Address Book.

Contact information may change, and you need to keep track of it and update your address book so that you have the latest information. Using various options in the Outlook Address Book, you can update the contact information with ease.

How to Update Contacts

Procedure Reference: Edit Contact Information

To edit the information of a contact:

1. Double-click a contact to display the contact information in a Contact form.
2. Edit the contact information.
   - In the Contact form, edit or enter information.
   - If necessary, on the **Contact** tab, in the **Show** group, click **Details** and in the Details form, edit or enter information.
3. Save the contact information and close the Contact form.

Procedure Reference: Add a Document or a Message to a Contact

To add a document or a message to a contact:

1. Open the desired contact for which you want to add information.
2. Add the desired information.
   - Add a document to a contact.
     a. On the **Insert** tab, in the **Include** group, click **Attach File.**
     b. In the **Insert File** dialog box, navigate to a folder and select a file.
     c. Click **Insert.**
   - If necessary, add an item to a contact.
     a. On the **Insert** tab, in the **Include** group, click **Outlook Item.**
     b. In the **Insert Item** dialog box, select the folder where you have the item.
     c. In the **Items** list box, select the desired item which you want to insert and click **OK.**
3. On the **Contact** tab, in the **Actions** group, click **Save & Close.**
4. If necessary, open the Contacts folder and check whether the document, Outlook item, or the message is added to the desired contact.

Procedure Reference: Add a Picture to a Contact Through the Insert Tab

To add a picture to a contact through the **Insert** tab:

1. Open a desired contact.
2. In the Contact form, click in the **Notes** area.

You can add a picture through the **Insert** tab only to the **Notes** area.

3. On the **Insert** tab, in the **Illustrations** group, click **Picture** to display the **Insert Picture** dialog box.
4. In the **Insert Picture** dialog box, navigate to a folder, select a picture, and click **Insert** to insert the selected picture.
5. Save and close the Contact form.

Procedure Reference: Add a Picture to a Contact Through the Contact Tab

Add a picture to a contact through the **Contact** tab:

1. Open a contact.
2. Display the **Add Contact Picture** dialog box.
   - On the **Contact** tab, in the **Options** group, from the **Picture** drop-down list, select **Add Picture** or;
   - In the Contact form, to the right of the **Full Name** text box, click the contact picture place holder.
3. In the **Add Contact Picture** dialog box, navigate to a folder, select a picture, and click **OK** to add the picture to the image place holder and the business card.
4. Save and close the Contact form.

Procedure Reference: Send a Contact Through Email

To send a contact through email:

1. Open the contact that you want to send.
2. On the **Contact** tab, in the **Actions** group, from the **Forward** drop-down list, select the desired option.
   - Select **As a Business Card** to send the Contact form as a business card with the name, job title, company, contact number, and email address.
   - Select **In Internet Format (vCard)** to send the Contact form as a vCard with the name and phone number.
   - Select **As an Outlook Contact** to send the Contact form as a contact attached to a Message form.
3. In the new Message form, type the desired user name and subject.
4. In the Message form, click **Send** to send the message.

Procedure Reference: Save a Contact Received as a Contact Record

To save a contact received as a contact record:

1. If necessary, open the Inbox.
2. Open the message with which the contact record is attached.
3. Right-click the attached contact record and select **Add to Outlook Contacts.**
4. On the **Contact** tab, in the **Actions** group, click **Save & Close.**

Procedure Reference: Delete a Contact

To delete a contact:

1. Open the Contacts folder.
2. Delete a contact.
   - Select a contact, and on the **Home** tab, in the **Delete** group, click **Delete** or;
   - Right-click the contact and choose **Delete** or;
   - Open the contact, and on the **Contact** tab, in the **Actions** group, click **Delete**.

Retrieving Contacts

The contacts that are deleted cannot be retrieved. The **Undo** command cannot be used to recover deleted contacts.

Procedure Reference: Print Contact Information

To print contact information:

1. On the Quick Launch bar, select **Contacts.**
2. Select the **File** tab and choose **Print** to display the print options in the Backstage view.
3. In the **Settings** section, select a print style.
4. In the **Printer** section, click **Print Options** to display the **Print** dialog box.
5. In the **Print** dialog box, set the desired print options.
6. Click **Print** to print information on contacts.

ACTIVITY 4-7
Editing a Contact

Data Files:

C:\084595Data\Managing Contacts\Melissa.jpg

Scenario:

Melissa Lang, a job applicant who was listed with your placement agency, was hired as a Programmer by the Citizens Info organization. Her email address is now mlang@citizensinfo.com. Her manager's name is Beth Hilton. You also have a photo of her. Your agency has a policy that all contact information must be kept up-to-date.

1. Update Melissa's job title, company, and email address.

    a. In the View pane, scroll up and double-click the business card of Mellisa Lang to open a Contact form with her information.

    b. In the **Company** text box, click and type *Citizens Info* and press **Tab.**

    c. In the **Job Title** text box, double-click the text "Applicant" and type *Programmer*

    d. In the **Internet** section, in the **E-mail** text box, click and type *mlang@citizensinfo.org*

2. Add the name of Melissa's manager.

    a. On the **Contact** tab, in the **Show** group, click **Details.**

    b. In the **Detail** form, in the **Manager's name** text box, click and type *Beth Hilton*

    c. On the **Contact** tab, in the **Show** group, click **General** to display the general view of the contact.

3. Add the picture to the contact.

a. In the Contact form, click the **Add Contact Picture** place holder to display the **Add Contact Picture** dialog box.

b. In the **Add Contact Picture** dialog box, navigate to the C:\084595 Data\Managing Contacts folder.

c. Select **Melissa.jpg** and click **OK** to insert the picture in the place holder.

d. On the **Contact** tab, in the **Actions** group, click **Save & Close.**

ACTIVITY 4-8
Working with Contacts

Scenario:
Your colleague has requested that you send contact information of some contacts. You decide to send the contact information as business cards, through email. You also need to save contact information that you have received by email in your Contacts folder. Finally, as you are going out of the office for a few days, you decide to print some contact information to take them with you.

1. Attach contact details as a business card.

   a. In the Contacts folder, scroll up and double-click the business card of Andy Bloom to open a Contact form with the information for Andy Bloom.

   b. On the **Contact** tab, in the **Actions** group, from the **Forward** drop-down list, select **As a Business Card.**

   c. Observe that a Message form is displayed with the contact information attached as a business card.

   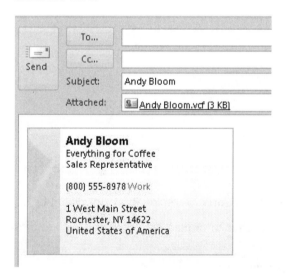

2. Send the message.

   a. In the Message form, in the **To** text box, type your partner's name and press **Tab.**

   b. In the **Subject** text box, triple-click and type *Contact information of Andy Bloom*

   c. Send the message and close the Contact form.

3. Save a contact received in an email as a contact record.

   a. Display the contents of the Inbox.

b. In the View pane, double-click the **Contact information** message.

c. In the Contact information — Message (HTML) window, in the message body right-click the business card and choose **Add To Outlook Contacts.**

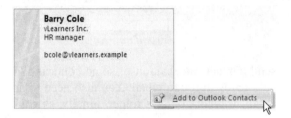

d. On the **Contact** tab, in the **Actions** group, click **Save & Close.**

e. Close the Contact information - Message (HTML) window.

4. Print the contacts.

   a. On the Quick Launch bar, select **Contacts.**

   b. Select the **File** tab and choose **Print.**

   c. In the **Settings** section, observe that **Card Style** is selected.

   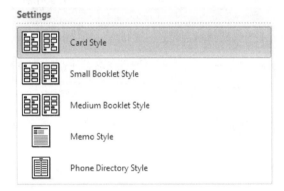

   d. In the **Printer** section, click **Print Options** to display the **Print** dialog box.

   e. In the **Copies** section, in the **Number of copies** spin box, click the up arrow to set the value to **2.**

   f. Click **Print** to print the contact information.

Lesson 4 Follow-up

In this lesson, you managed contacts. You can now store details of contacts along with their email addresses and organize them, so that you can easily retrieve the desired information.

1. **What are the details that can be stored in Outlook Contacts?**

2. **What are some custom category names that you may prefer to use for organizing your contacts?**

5 | Scheduling Appointments

Lesson Time: 35 minutes

Lesson Objectives:

In this lesson, you will schedule appointments.

You will:

- Explore the Outlook calendar.
- Schedule an appointment.
- Edit appointments.

Introduction

You managed contacts using the Outlook Address Book. In addition to using email and adding contacts, Outlook can also be used to keep track of your schedules. In this lesson, you will schedule appointments using Outlook.

Scheduling meetings and setting up reminders are integral to any business interaction. Outlook is an important tool for setting up and planning your business engagements. You can keep your schedules up-to-date and coordinate with associates and clients in the most efficient way.

TOPIC A
Explore the Outlook Calendar

You added and updated your contacts in Outlook. You also want to gain familiarity with the Outlook calendar to plan your meetings with contacts, and ensure that the scheduled meetings can be viewed in Outlook. In this topic, you will explore the Outlook calendar.

At work, scheduling day-to-day appointments to complete certain tasks is essential. You will certainly need help to schedule things that you want to do. Having chosen to use Outlook, it is important to familiarize yourself with the Outlook calendar before working with it.

The Outlook Calendar

The Outlook calendar is used for planning and scheduling appointments. The calendar has two main sections: **Date Navigator** and **Appointment**. The **Date Navigator** section displays the calendar for the current month, enabling you to quickly select a date to display or add items, and also allows you to navigate through the months and years. The **Appointment** section, which is divided into hourly time slots, displays all appointments for the day selected in the **Date Navigator.**

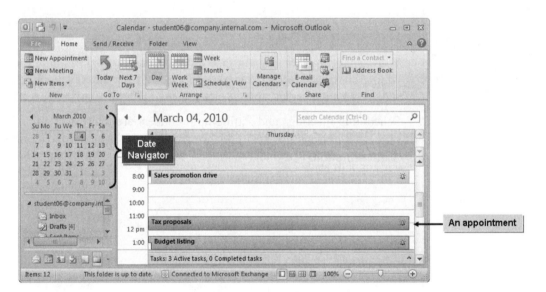

Figure 5-1: The Calendar listing various appointments.

Types of Calendar Entries

You can create different types of entries in a calendar.

Entry Type	Used to Reserve
New Appointment	A time slot for a designated purpose.
New Recurring Appointment	A time slot that is used more than once over a period of time for a designated purpose.
New All Day Event	A specific day or group of days for a designated purpose.
New Meeting Request	A time slot for a designated purpose involving other participants.
New Recurring Meeting Request	A time slot that is used more than once over a period of time for a designated purpose involving other participants.
New Recurring Event	A specific day or group of days used more than once over a period of time for a designated purpose involving other participants.

Calendar Views

In Outlook, you can choose to view the calendar in any of the four different formats. The Day view presents a detailed schedule for the selected day in hourly time slots. The Work Week view displays the five work days (Monday through Friday), split into hourly time slots. The Week view displays the entire week (Sunday through Saturday), representing each day in a boxed time slot. The Month view displays the selected month with **Low, Medium,** or **High** level of detail, but without any time slot for the days.

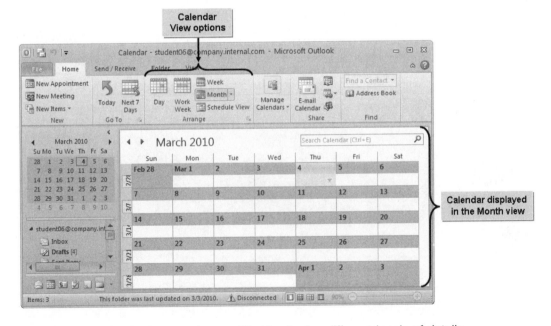

Figure 5-2: The Month view can be modified to display different levels of details.

The Schedule View

The Schedule view is an option available in the **Arrange** group on the **Home** tab. It helps you to view the calendar as a horizontal layout. It is also useful when you select multiple calendars to check and schedule appointments or meetings.

How to Explore the Outlook Calendar

Procedure Reference: Display the Outlook Calendar in Different Views

To display the Outlook calendar in different views:

1. On the Quick Launch bar, click **Calendar.**
2. On the **Home** tab, in the **Arrange** group, click a button to display the calendar in a different view.
   - Click **Day** to view the calendar for a day and with hourly time slots.
   - Click **Work Week** to view the calendar for a week with days between Monday and Friday.
   - Click **Week** to view the calendar for a week with days between Sunday and Saturday.
   - Click **Month** to view the calendar for a month.
3. If necessary, use the buttons in the **Go To** group.
   - On the Ribbon, in the **Go To** group, click **Today** to view the calendar for the current day.
   - Click **Next 7 days** to view the schedules for the next seven days.

ACTIVITY 5-1
Exploring the Outlook Calendar

Scenario:
You need to frequently use the Outlook calendar at work. Before you can begin using the calendar efficiently, it is a good idea to spend some time familiarizing yourself with the calendar environment.

1. Display the calendar in different views.

    a. On the Quick Launch bar, click **Calendar.**

    b. On the **Home** tab, in the **Arrange** group, click **Week.**

    c. Observe that the days of the week from Sunday through Saturday are displayed with time slots.

    d. On the **Home** tab, in the **Arrange** group, click **Work Week** to display the days of the work week from Monday through Friday with time slots.

    e. On the **Home** tab, in the **Arrange** group, click **Month** to display the current month without the time slots.

    f. In the Date Navigation section, select the upcoming Wednesday to view the selected day with time slots.

2. Use the buttons in the **Go To** group to view the calendar for the current day and the next seven days.

    a. On the **Home** tab, in the **Go To** group, click **Today** to view the day's calendar.

    b. Click **Next 7 Days** to show the next seven days in the calendar.

TOPIC B
Schedule an Appointment

You explored the Outlook calendar and are familiar with it. You can now use the calendar to track your schedules and keep track of appointments. In this topic, you will schedule an appointment using the Outlook calendar.

You may have multiple appointments and find it hard to keep track of all of them on paper or in memory. There is a possibility of forgetting an appointment or misplacing the paper. In business interactions, this creates a negative image and can be avoided by keeping track of your appointments and updating them regularly so that you do not miss important meetings. By using the Outlook calendar to track your appointments, you can avoid these types of predicaments.

The Appointment Form

The *Appointment form* allows you to enter any specific information or set options while scheduling an appointment. It can be launched from the **New** group on the **Home** tab. The **Appointment** tab in the form has different groups that help in scheduling appointments.

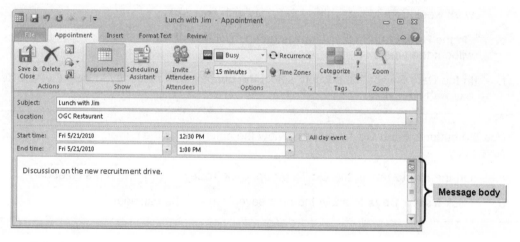

Figure 5-3: A new Appointment form displaying the various components to schedule an appointment.

The Appointment form has various components that allow you to enter the details of an appointment.

Component	Allows You To
Subject text box	Enter a brief description of the appointment.
Location text box	Enter the location where the appointment will be held.
Start time drop-down lists	Select or enter the date and time when the appointment starts.
End time drop-down lists	Select or enter the date and time when the appointment ends.

Component	Allows You To
All day vent check box	Specify whether the appointment is scheduled for the whole day.
Message body	Enter information about the appointment.

Calendar Symbols

Items on the calendar have symbols to convey the status of scheduled appointments and to help you determine your schedule at a glance.

Symbol	Indicates That
↻	The appointment will recur in the future.
🔒	The appointment is private.

How to Schedule an Appointment

Procedure Reference: Launch a New Appointment Form

To launch a new Appointment form:

1. In the Navigation pane, click **Calendar** to display the calendar.

    It is essential to display the calendar in the Day view for you to schedule appointments for a single day. If the calendar is in the Week view, the whole week gets selected in the **Date Navigator**.

2. In the **Date Navigator** section, select a suitable date.
3. Launch the Appointment form.
   - On the **Home** tab, in the **New** group, click **New Appointment** or;
   - On the **Home** tab, in the **New** group, from the **New Items** drop-down list, select **Appointment** or;
   - In the calendar, double-click the day on which the appointment is to be set or;
   - In the calendar, right-click the day on which the appointment is to be set and choose **New Appointment**.

Procedure Reference: Schedule an Appointment

To schedule an appointment:

1. Display an Appointment form.

2. In the Appointment form, type the necessary details.
   - In the **Subject** text box, type a subject of your choice.
   - In the **Location** text box, type the location for the appointment.
   - From the **Start Time** drop-down lists, select the desired date and time.
   - From the **End Time** drop-down lists, select the desired date and time.
   - If necessary, check the **All Day Event** check box to specify that the scheduled appointment is to occur throughout the day.
3. If necessary, on the **Appointment** tab, set additional options for the appointment.
   - In the **Attendees** group, click **Invite Attendees** and in the Message form that opens, fill in the necessary details and send the message to the invitees.
   - In the **Options** group, from the **Reminder** drop-down list, select a time at which you want to be reminded about the appointment.
   - If necessary, in the **Options** group, from the **Show As** drop-down list, select an option to set the availability status for your appointment.
     - Select **Free** to show your status as free to attend the appointment.
     - Select **Tentative** to show that you may not be available for the appointment.
     - Select **Busy** to show that you will be busy during the scheduled time.
     - Select **Out of Office** to show that you will not be available at the office during the scheduled time.
4. On the **Appointment** tab, in the **Actions** group, click **Save & Close** to save and close the appointment.

Appointment Reminders

An appointment reminder is a visual and auditory alarm notifying you that you have an appointment. By default, each scheduled appointment has a reminder of 15 minutes.

Recurring Appointments

A scheduled appointment that is supposed to occur repeatedly at the specified timings over a period of time is called a recurring appointment.

Procedure Reference: Create a Recurring Appointment

To create a recurring appointment:
1. Open an Appointment form.
2. Enter the details in the Appointment form.
3. On the **Appointment** tab, in the **Options** group, click **Recurrence** to display the **Appointment Recurrence** dialog box.

4. In the **Appointment Recurrence** dialog box, set the options to define the recurrence of the appointment.
   - In the **Appointment time** section, specify the start and end time of the appointment.
   - In the **Recurrence pattern** section, specify whether the appointment has a daily, weekly, monthly or yearly recurrence.
   - In the **Range of Recurrence** section, from the **Start** drop-down list, select the desired date on which the appointment will start to recur.
   - In the **Range of Recurrence** section, from the **End by** drop-down list, select the desired date on which the appointment will end and will not recur there after.
   - In the **End after** text box, click and type the desired number of appointments after which the appointment will cease to occur.
5. Click **OK** to close the dialog box and return to the Appointment form.
6. Save and close the appointment.

Procedure Reference: Create an Appointment from an Email Message

To create an appointment from an email message:

1. In the View pane, right-click the message that you need to create an appointment from and choose **Move→Other Folder** to display the **Move Items** dialog box.
2. In the **Move Items** dialog box, in the **Move the selected items to the folder** section, select **Calendar** and click **OK.**
3. An Appointment form is opened with the subject from the email message and the message text mentioned in the message body. Select the appropriate starting date and time for the appointment.
4. Select the appropriate ending date and time for the appointment.
5. In the **Location** text box, type the desired location.
6. If necessary, check the **All Day Event** check box to specify that the appointment is a day-long event.
7. On the **Appointment** tab, in the **Attendees** group, click **Invite Attendees** to display the Message form.
8. In the **To** text box, fill in the name of the recipient.
9. Click **Send** to send the invitation. The email message will be moved from the folder it was in to the calendar and saved as an appointment.

Appointments from Email Messages

When you create an appointment from an email message, you need to move the message to the calendar folder. When this is done, a new Appointment form opens with the content of the email message displayed as the message body of the appointment. After filling in the necessary details in the Appointment form, you can send it to the attendees. Once the appointment is sent, the email message from which the appointment was created will be stored in the calendar folder.

ACTIVITY 5-2
Scheduling Appointments

Scenario:

You just made plans to meet a friend, the coming Friday, between 12 and 1 PM, and have also scheduled an appointment this Saturday from 1 PM to 2 PM with your dentist. Your company is shortly hosting a recruitment conference. You have been given charge of organizing the conference and have decided to hold team conference calls for the next six weeks, on Fridays, from 10 AM to 11 AM.

1. Display a new Appointment form to fix an appointment for the coming Friday.

   a. In the Date Navigator section, click the date of the coming Friday.

   b. On the **Home** tab, in the **New** group, click **New Appointment** to open an Appointment form.

2. Enter a subject and location for the appointment.

   a. Maximize the Appointment form.

   b. In the **Subject** text box, type *Lunch with Jim* and press **Tab.**

   c. In the **Location** text box, type *Coffee House*

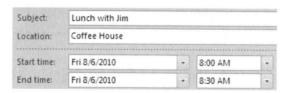

3. Set the appointment time.

   a. In the second **Start Time** drop-down list, scroll down and select **12:00 PM.**

   b. From the second **End Time** drop-down list, select **1:00 PM (1 hour).**

   c. On the **Appointment** tab, in the **Actions** group, click **Save & Close.**

4. Create an appointment for a consultation with your dentist this Saturday.

   a. In the Date Navigator section, select this Saturday's date.

   b. On the **Home** tab, in the **New** group, click **New Appointment** to open a new Appointment form.

   c. In the **Subject** text box, type *Visit to dentist*

   d. In the second **Start Time** drop-down list, scroll down and select **1:00 PM.**

e. From the second **End Time** drop-down list, select **2:00 PM (1 hour)**.

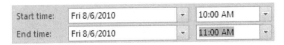

f. On the **Appointment** tab, in the **Actions** group, click **Save & Close**.

5. Create a one-hour appointment for a Recruitment Conference Call.

   a. In the Date Navigator section, select the upcoming Friday's date.

   b. Display a new Appointment form.

   c. In the new Appointment form, in the **Subject** text box, type *Recruitment Conference Call*

   d. From the second **Start Time** drop-down list, select **10:00 AM**.

   e. From the second **End Time** drop-down list, select **11:00 AM (1 hour)**.

6. Set the **Recurrence** option so that the appointment occurs on a weekly basis for six weeks.

   a. On the **Appointment** tab, in the **Options** group, click **Recurrence** to display the **Appointment Recurrence** dialog box.

   b. In the **Appointment Recurrence** dialog box, in the **Recurrence pattern** section, observe that the **Weekly** option is selected.

   c. In the **Range of recurrence** section, in the **End after** text box, double-click the value and type *6* to end the recurrence after six such appointments.

   d. Click **OK** to return to the Appointment form.

   e. Observe the details of the recurring appointment.

   f. On the **Appointment Series** tab, in the **Actions** group, click **Save & Close**.

7. View the recurring appointment by using the Month view.

   a. On the **Home** tab, in the **Arrange** group, click **Month** to view the recurrence of the Recruitment Conference Call appointment in the calendar.

b. Observe that the team meeting appointment recurs on consecutive Fridays starting from the day you scheduled the appointment.

c. In the Month view, to the left of the month and year at the top of the pane, click the **Forward** button, which is placed second from the left to view the calendar for the next month.

d. Observe that the team meeting is also scheduled for Fridays in the upcoming month.

e. On the **Home** tab, in the **Go To** group, click **Today** to return to the current month view.

ACTIVITY 5-3
Creating an Appointment from an Email Message

Scenario:
You have received an email from your manager, informing you about an interview schedule. You want to get into a detailed discussion regarding this email with your manager.

1. Open an Appointment form from an email message.

    a. On the Quick Launch bar, click **Mail**.

    b. In the View pane, right-click the **Recruitment of candidates** message and choose **Move→Other Folder**.

    c. In the **Move Items** dialog box, in the **Move the selected items to the folder** list box, select **Calendar** and click **OK**.

    d. Observe that a new Appointment form is opened with the Recruitment of candidates message attached to the message body.

    Recruitment of candidates

2. Schedule and send an appointment.

    a. In the **Location** text box, type **Conference Room**

    b. From the first **Start Time** drop-down list, select the upcoming Thursday.

    c. From the second **Start Time** drop-down list, scroll down and select **4.00 PM.**

    d. From the second **End Time** drop-down list, verify that the time corresponding to 30 minutes from the start time is selected.

    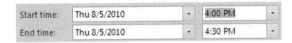

    e. On the **Appointment** tab, in the **Actions** group, click **Save & Close**.

TOPIC C
Edit Appointments

You scheduled appointments using the Outlook calendar. You may want to reschedule appointments or prioritize them based on their importance. In this topic, you will edit appointments.

You may have some appointments in the calendar that you do not want to miss. It may also contain appointments that you want to assign as having the least priority. Some other appointments may need to be edited and rescheduled depending upon your need. By editing and organizing your appointments, you can easily manage them.

The Private Appointments Option

Outlook enables you to mark an appointment **Private** so that others will not be able to open and view it when the calendar is shared. Private appointments are indicated by a lock symbol beside them.

How to Edit Appointments

Procedure Reference: Assign a Color Category to an Appointment

To assign a color category to an appointment:

1. Open the appointment for which you want to assign a category.
   - Double-click the appointment or;
   - Select the appointment, and on the **Calendar Tools** tool tab, on the **Appointment Series** contextual tab, in the **Actions** group, click **Open.**

2. In the Appointment form, on the **Appointment** tab, in the **Tags** group, from the **Categorize** drop-down list, select the desired category.
   - Select an existing category or;
   - Select **All Categories** to open the **Color Categories** dialog box. In the dialog box, create a color category.

3. Save and close the appointment.

Procedure Reference: Assign a Color Category to a Recurring Appointment

To assign a color category to a recurring appointment:

1. Open a recurring appointment to display the **Open Recurring Item** dialog box.
2. In the **Open Recurring Item** dialog box, select the **Open the Series** option and click **OK.**

Outlook does not allow you to assign a color category for a single occurrence of a recurring appointment.

3. In the Appointment form, from the **Categorize** drop-down list, select the desired category to assign a color category to all the occurrences of the appointment.
4. If necessary, in the **Rename Category** dialog box, in the **Name** text box, enter the desired name for the category, and click **Yes.**

5. Save and close the appointment.

Procedure Reference: Edit an Appointment

To edit an appointment:
1. Open the Appointment form of the appointment you want to edit.
2. Make the appropriate edits in the Appointment form.
   - From the **Start Time** drop-down lists, select the desired time and date, respectively.
   - From the **End Time** drop-down lists, select the desired time and date, respectively.
   - If necessary, modify the subject and the location.
   - On the **Appointment** tab, in the **Tags** group, from the **Categorize** drop-down list, select a color category to categorize the appointment.

    You can set other options such as **Rooms, Reminder, Show As,** and **Invite Attendees.**

3. On the **Appointment** tab, in the **Actions** group, click **Save & Close**.

Procedure Reference: Mark an Appointment Private

To mark an appointment private:
1. Open an existing appointment or a new Appointment form.
2. If necessary, specify the information for the appointment.
3. In the Appointment form, on the **Appointment** tab, in the **Tags** group, click **Private** to mark the appointment private.
4. On the **Appointment** tab, in the **Actions** group, click **Save & Close**.

Delete an Appointment

There are different ways to delete an appointment.
- Right-click the appointment and choose **Delete** or;
- Open the appointment and on the **Appointment** tab, in the **Actions** group, click **Delete**.

ACTIVITY 5-4
Assigning Categories and Marking Appointments Private

Scenario:
You want to display similar appointments together in the calendar, so that at a glance you can identify these appointments. Further, Jim called to tell you that he cannot make it to lunch on Friday from 12 – 1 PM. He wants to meet from 1:30 PM to 2:30 PM instead. In addition to this change, you have also decided to mark your lunch appointment as private so that your coworkers can view it, but not open it.

1. Assign the **Personal** category to the Lunch with Jim appointment.

    a. On the Quick Launch bar, click **Calendar.**

    b. On the **Home** tab, in the **Arrange** group, click **Day.**

    c. In the Date Navigator section, in the calendar, select the upcoming Friday.

    d. In the Day view of the calendar, double-click the **Lunch with Jim** appointment to open an Appointment form with the details of this appointment.

    e. On the **Appointment** tab, in the **Tags** group, from the **Categorize** drop-down list, select **All Categories.**

    f. In the **Color Categories** dialog box, check the **Green Category** check box and click **Rename.**

    g. Type *Personal* to rename the **Green Category** and click **OK.**

h. Observe the green color bar displayed at the top of the Appointment form indicating that the appointment is categorized as **Personal.**

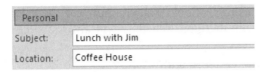

2. Change the Lunch with Jim appointment's start time and mark it private.

   a. In the Appointment form, from the second **Start Time** drop-down list, select **1:30 PM.**

   b. Observe that the end time for the appointment automatically changes to **2:30 PM.**

   c. On the **Appointment** tab, in the **Tags** group, click the **Private** button, to mark the Lunch with Jim appointment as a private one.

   d. In the **Actions** group, click **Save & Close** and observe that a lock symbol appears at the right end of the Lunch with Jim appointment indicating that the appointment is marked private.

3. Assign the **Business** category to the Recruitment Conference Call appointment.

   a. In the Day view of the calendar select the **Recruitment Conference Call** appointment.

   b. On the **Calendar Tools** tool tab, on the **Appointment Series** contextual tab, in the **Tags** group, from the **Categorize** drop-down list, select **Business.**

   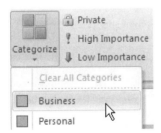

   c. Observe that the Recruitment Conference Call appointment is now assigned the **Business** category.

Lesson 5: Scheduling Appointments

Lesson 5 Follow-up

In this lesson, you scheduled appointments using Outlook. You can now use the calendar to keep track of all your appointments and ensure that your schedule will always be up-to-date and easy to read.

1. **Which calendar view would you prefer to work with? Why?**

2. **How useful is the Appointment form when you schedule appointments?**

6 | Managing Meetings in Outlook

Lesson Time: 1 hour(s), 20 minutes

Lesson Objectives:

In this lesson, you will schedule a meeting.

You will:

- Schedule a meeting.
- Respond to a meeting request.
- Manage meetings by tracking the response and rescheduling them.
- Print the Outlook calendar.

Introduction

You used the Outlook calendar to schedule and track your appointments. Unlike appointments, meetings involve multiple participants who need to be informed. In this lesson, you will learn how to schedule a meeting.

Meetings are inevitable in any professional interaction. Some meetings are unpremeditated, but often you are faced with the task of scheduling a meeting, determining its participants, notifying them, booking resources, and securing a location. Outlook enables you to do all these tasks and more, including tracking the attendance of participants.

TOPIC A
Schedule a Meeting

You tracked appointments using Outlook. When you schedule a meeting, you need to involve multiple participants and notify all of them. In this topic, you will schedule a meeting.

You may have to schedule a department meeting. You could invite the participants by phone, but that would take some time, especially if someone is not available by phone. By scheduling a meeting in Outlook, you can quickly invite the participants and allocate resources, and you can choose a time slot that is convenient for everyone.

Scheduling a Meeting

In Outlook, scheduling a meeting is a process in itself:

1. You send a meeting invitation to all identified participants.
2. The meeting is automatically entered in your calendar.
3. Recipients open the meeting request and respond by accepting, tentatively accepting, or declining the invitation, or they may respond by proposing a new time.
4. If accepted, the meeting is added to the recipient's calendar.
5. A mail is sent to you stating the recipient's response.

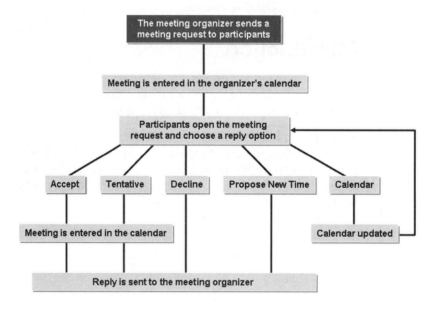

Figure 6-1: Scheduling a meeting in Outlook.

The Meeting Form

The Meeting form is a window used for scheduling meetings. You can launch the form by clicking the **New Meeting** button on the **Home** tab. This form contains various fields and components that can be used for entering specific information relating to a meeting.

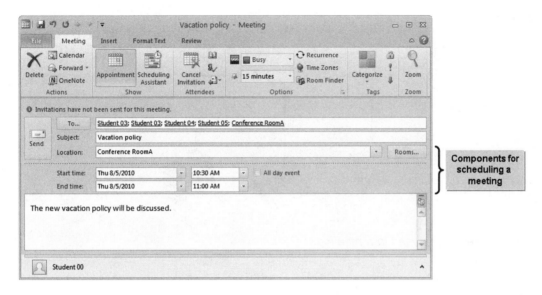

Figure 6-2: A meeting form for scheduling meetings.

Component	Allows You To
To text box	Enter the name of the recipient.
To button	Display the **Select Attendees and Resources: Global Address List.**
Send button	Send the meeting invitation to the intended recipient.
Subject text box	Enter a brief description of the meeting.
Location text box	Enter the location where the meeting will be held.
Rooms button	Select a room where the meeting will be held.
Start Time drop-down lists	Enter the start date and time.
End Time drop-down lists	Enter the end date and time.
All Day Event checkbox	Specify whether the meeting is scheduled for the whole day.
Message text area	Enter any additional information about the meeting.

Meeting Resources

Definition:

Meeting resources are facilities and equipment used in a meeting. For example: rooms, projectors, stationery and other such items that are usually arranged in advance.

Example:

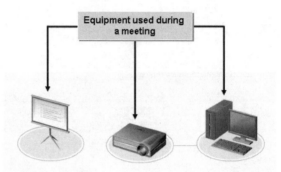

Figure 6-3: Resources used in a meeting.

The Room Finder Pane

The **Room Finder** pane helps you to locate a room for a meeting. It consists of a calendar and the **Choose an available room** and **Suggested times** list boxes. When you select a date in the Meeting form, the **Room Finder** pane displays the available rooms to choose from. The pane also indicates the chances of getting a room using three levels—**Good, Fair, and Poor.** The **Suggested times** list box displays a list of suggested times for a meeting.

The Scheduling Assistant

The Scheduling Assistant helps you to identify the free or busy status of resources, and enables you to confirm the availability of participants for a meeting. In the **Room Finder** pane, the **Suggested times** list box displays a list of suggested times for a meeting based on the availability information of specified resources. The Scheduling Assistant can be accessed from the **Show** group of the **Meeting** tab on the Meeting form.

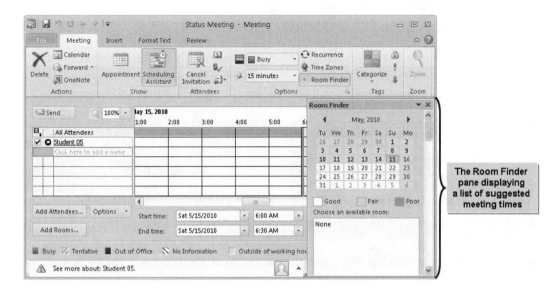

Figure 6-4: The Scheduling Assistant used to book resources.

Calendar Attendant

A Calendar Attendant processes meeting requests as and when they are scheduled, whether or not you are logged on through Outlook or another mail server. It is a feature that automatically places new meetings as tentative appointments on the Calendar, updates meetings, and deletes meetings that are completed.

Resource Booking Attendant

The **Resource Booking Attendant** automates the process of accepting or declining resource booking requests. This feature basically works by setting policies for automating the resource booking requests. Policies can be set to book each individual resource.

Scheduling Smartly Using Outlook 2010

The **Scheduling Assistant, Calendar Attendant,** and **Resource Booking Attendant** are part of the Microsoft Outlook 2010 smart scheduling functionality. The **Scheduling Assistant** feature helps you to identify the free or busy status of multiple people at the same time, and enables you to confirm the availability of participants. It also displays suggested times and rooms indicating the availability of the resources specified. The **Calendar Attendant** feature helps to manage your Calendar and ensures that time slots are not overbooked; the **Resource Booking Attendant** feature helps you to manage the process of accepting and declining of resource booking requests.

How to Schedule a Meeting

Procedure Reference: Schedule a Meeting

To schedule a meeting:

1. In the Date Navigator section, select the date of the meeting.
2. If necessary, in the **Appointment** section, click the time you want the meeting to start.

 You can also select the date and time in the **Meeting** form.

3. Open a **New Meeting** form.
   - On the **Home** tab, in the **New** group, click **New Meeting** to open a new meeting form or;
   - On the **Home** tab, in the **New** group, from the **New Items** drop-down list, select **Meeting.**
4. In the Meeting form, enter the subject, start time, and end time for the meeting.
5. Specify the attendees and resources for the meeting.
   a. In the Meeting form, click **To,** to display the **Select Attendees And Resources: Global Address List** dialog box.
   b. In the **Select Attendees And Resources: Global Address List** dialog box, in the list box, select the appropriate attendees.
   c. Click **Required** to add the selected user names to the **Required** text box.
   d. If necessary, select the attendees and click **Optional** to invite optional attendees to the meeting.
   e. Click **OK** to return to the Meeting form.

 You can also type the user names of the attendees directly in the **To** text box, separating each user name with a comma.

6. If necessary, book rooms for meetings.
   - Specify the rooms from the **Global Address List.**
     a. In the **Select Attendees And Resources: Global Address List** dialog box, in the Meeting form, click **To** to display the **Select Attendees And Resources: Global Address List** dialog box.
     b. In the list box, select the appropriate rooms.
     c. Click **Resources** to add the selected **Conference Rooms** to the **Resources** text box and click **OK.**
   - Specify the rooms in the Meeting form.
     a. In the **Meeting** form, click **Rooms.**
     b. In the **Select Rooms: All Rooms** dialog box, select the appropriate rooms.
     c. Click **Rooms** to add the selected rooms to the **Rooms** text box and click **OK.**
7. On the **Meeting** tab, in the **Show** group, click **Scheduling Assistant** to check the availability of the attendees.

8. The calendar details of all attendees are displayed in the **Scheduling Assistant** view of the **Meeting** form. Scroll to the right or left to view the status of each attendee.
9. If necessary, select the desired options in the **Meeting** form.
   - Remove the check mark of an attendee to remove the attendee from the meeting invitation.
   - Click **Add Attendees** and select the users, resources, and facilities from the **Select Attendees And Resources: Global Address List** dialog box.
   - Click **Add Rooms** and select the room to specify the location of the meeting.
   - Select the start and end time from the **Start time** and **End time** drop-down lists, respectively.
10. Click **Options** and choose your desired selection:
    - **Show Only My Working Hours** to only display the working hours of all the users.
    - **Show Calendar Details** to display all Calendar items of the group members except the items marked private.
    - **Refresh Free/Busy** to connect to the free/busy server and obtain all the free/busy information about the group members.
11. In the **Meeting** form, click **Send** to send the meeting request.

Procedure Reference: Schedule a Recurring Meeting

To schedule a recurring meeting:
1. Open a new Meeting form.
2. Enter the details in the Meeting form.
3. On the **Meeting** tab, in the **Options** group, click **Occurrence.**
4. In the **Appointment Recurrence** dialog box, set the options to define the recurrence of the appointment.
   - In the **Appointment time** section, specify the start and end time of the appointment.
   - In the **Recurrence pattern** section, specify whether the appointment has a daily, weekly, monthly or yearly recurrence.
   - In the **Range of Recurrence** section, from the **Start** drop-down list, select the desired date on which the appointment will recur.
   - In the **Range of Recurrence** section, from the **End by** drop-down list, select the desired date on which the appointment will end and will not recur thereafter.
   - In the **End after** text box, click and type the desired number of appointments after which the appointment will cease to occur.
5. Click **OK** to close the dialog box and return to the Appointment form.
6. Save and close the meeting.

Procedure Reference: Mark a Meeting Private

To mark a meeting private:
1. In the Date Navigator section, select the date of the meeting.
2. In the **Appointment** section, click the time you want the meeting to start.
3. Open a new Meeting form. You can also open an already existing Meeting form and set it as a private meeting.

4. In the Meeting form, enter the desired subject, location, attendees, end time, and optional attendees and resources.
5. On the **Meeting** tab, in the **Tags** group, click the **Private** to set the meeting as private.
6. In the Meeting form, click **Send** to send the meeting request.

Procedure Reference: Schedule a Meeting from an Email Message

To schedule a meeting from an email message:

1. In the Inbox, open the message for which you need to create a meeting.
2. In the displayed message window, on the **Message** tab, in the **Respond** group, click **Meeting** to reply with a meeting.
3. A new Meeting form is opened with the attendees in the **To** text box, and the subject displayed in the **Subject** text box. Select the appropriate start and end dates and the time for the meeting.
4. Enter the desired location.
5. If necessary, set the meeting as recurring.
6. If necessary, enter the optional attendees and resources.
7. In the Meeting form, click **Send** to send the meeting request.

ACTIVITY 6-1
Scheduling a Meeting

Scenario:
The new vacation policy was discussed in the managers' meeting. The managers need to meet with their staff to discuss possible options for a new vacation policy and request input. Your manager has asked you to schedule a meeting with him the following week. You also need to book the resources for the meeting.

1. Display a Meeting form for the upcoming Tuesday at 10.00 A.M.

    a. In the Date Navigator section, select the upcoming Tuesday's date.

    b. In the Day view of the calendar, select the top half of the 10 A.M. time slot.

    c. On the **Home** tab, in the **New** group, click **New Meeting.**

    d. In the Meeting form, observe that the start and end time is set to 10 A.M. and 10:30 A.M., respectively.

2. Select the participants.

    a. In the Meeting form, click **To**

    b. In the **Select Attendees And Resources: Global List** dialog box, in the list box, select **student00.**

    c. Click **Required** to place the selected user name in the **Required** text box and click **OK.**

3. Reserve Conference Room A.

    a. In the Meeting form, to the right of the **Location** text box, click **Rooms.**

    b. In the **Select Rooms: All Rooms** dialog box, in the list box, verify that **Conference Room A** is selected and then click **Rooms** to place the selected conference room in the **Rooms** text box.

c. Click **OK** to return to the Meeting form.

4. Enter the subject and send the meeting request.

   a. In the **Subject** text box, click and type *Vacation policy*

   b. On the **Meeting** tab, in the **Show** group, click **Scheduling Assistant** to view the time and availability of a meeting resource.

   c. Verify that the calendar details of the attendees are displayed in the Scheduling Assistant view of the Meeting form and that all the invited attendees are available.

5. Mark the meeting private.

   a. On the **Meeting** tab, in the **Tags** group, click **Private**.

   b. In the Meeting form, click **Send** to send the meeting request.

   c. In the Day view, verify that the meeting is displayed with a lock symbol.

ACTIVITY 6-2
Scheduling a Recurring Meeting

Scenario:
You have been assigned to train new recruits in your organization. You decide to schedule training sessions every Wednesday at 4.00 P.M. in Conference Room B for the next four weeks.

1. Schedule a meeting for next Wednesday at 4:00 P.M.

    a. In the Date Navigator section, select the next Wednesday's date.

    b. In the Day view of the calendar, scroll down and select the top half of the 4.00 P.M. tine slot.

    c. On the **Home** tab, in the **New** group, click **New Meeting**.

2. Invite the attendees to attend the meeting in Conference Room B.

    a. In the Meeting form, click **To**.

    b. In the **Select Attendees And Resources: Global Address List** dialog box, select your partner's user name.

    c. If necessary, hold down **Ctrl** and select three additional user names.

    d. Click **Required** and click **OK** to return to the Meeting form.

    e. In the Meeting form, click **Rooms**.

    f. In the **Select Rooms : All Rooms** dialog box, in the list box, select **Conference Room B**.

    g. Click **Rooms** and then click **OK** to return to the Meeting form.

    h. In the **Subject** text box, click and type *Training*

3. Schedule the meeting to recur every Wednesday for the next four weeks.

    a. On the **Meeting** tab, in the **Options** group, click **Recurrence**.

b. In the **Appointment Recurrence** dialog box, in the **Range of recurrence** section, in the **End after** text box, double-click **10** and type **4**

c. Click **OK,** and in the Meeting form, click **Send.**

ACTIVITY 6-3
Scheduling a Meeting from an Email Message

Scenario:
You received an email from your manager about the new vacation policy. You wanted to discuss this with him in detail.

1. Create a meeting request from the Vacation policy issues message and set the location.

    a. Select the **Inbox,** and in the View pane, double-click the **Vacation policy issues** message.

    b. On the **Message** tab, in the **Respond** group, click **Meeting.**

    c. Verify that a Meeting form is displayed with the subject **Vacation policy issues** in the **Subject** text box.

    d. Click **Rooms.**

    e. In the **Select Rooms: All Rooms** dialog box, in the list box, select **Conference Room C** and click **Rooms.**

    f. Click **OK** to return to the Meeting form.

2. Set the meeting times and send the request.

    a. In the Meeting form, from the first **Start time** drop-down list, select the upcoming Monday.

    b. From the second **Start time** drop-down list, select 10.00 A.M.

    c. From the second **End Time** drop-down list, select the time with an interval of 1 hour.

    d. In the message body, click and type *We can have a discussion on this issue.*

    e. In the Meeting form, click **Send.**

    f. Close the Vacation policy issues message.

TOPIC B
Reply to a Meeting Request

You know how to schedule a meeting. Often when you receive an invitation, you will want to respond with your availability status for the meeting or propose a new meeting time. In this topic, you will reply to a meeting request.

You may receive a meeting request. By using Outlook to reply to the meeting request, the organizer can be assured of your attendance or absence from the meeting. If you need to decline the invitation, you could compose a new email message suggesting an alternate meeting time. However, that can take some time and possibly involve a lot of back and forth email messages. To save time, you can propose a new time for the meeting directly from the invitation.

Responses

Outlook provides you with several invitation response options to choose from.

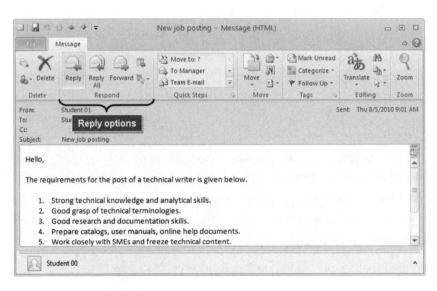

Figure 6-5: Reply options in Outlook.

Response Options	Description
Accept	Accept the meeting invite.
Tentative	Tentatively accept the meeting invite.
Decline	Decline the meeting invite.
Propose New Time	Either tentatively accept the invite and propose a new meeting time, or decline the invite and propose a new meeting time.
Respond	Provide options to reply, reply to all, and forward to the intended recipients.

Calendar Preview

When a message with an invitation for an event is received, Outlook displays the event details along with the date and time slots as part of the email message in the Reading pane. This allows you to preview the date of the event and respond to it without having to open the message.

How to Respond to a Meeting Request

Procedure Reference: Respond to a Meeting Request

To accept or decline a meeting request:

1. In the Inbox, open the meeting request message.
2. If necessary, on the **Meeting** tab, in the **Calendar** group, click **Calendar** to check your calendar.
3. If necessary, click **Close** to close the calendar.
4. Accept or decline a meeting request.
   - Accept the meeting request.
     a. On the **Meeting** tab, in the **Respond** group, from the **Accept** drop-down list, select the desired option.
     b. Click **OK** to send the response.
     c. Right-click the **Meeting** request and choose **Accept,** and then choose the desired option. Click **OK.**

     You could choose to edit the response before sending it, or accept without sending a response.

   - Decline the meeting request.
     a. On the **Meeting** tab, in the **Respond** group, from the **Decline** drop-down list, select the desired declining option.
     b. Click **OK** to edit the response before sending.

     You could choose to send the response without editing it, or decline without sending a response.

     c. In the **Message Body** of the **Response** form, type a response.
5. In the Meeting form, click **Send.**

Meeting Conflicts

When you open a meeting request that conflicts with another appointment on your Calendar, Outlook alerts you by displaying a warning in the InfoBar. Conflicting meetings are displayed adjacent to each other on the Calendar.

Procedure Reference: Propose a New Meeting Time

To propose a new meeting time:

1. In the Inbox, open the meeting request message.

2. On the **Meeting** tab, in the **Respond** group, from the **Propose New Time** drop-down list, select **Tentative And Propose New Time** or **Decline And Propose New Time.**
3. Set desired options, such as the start and end dates and times, or click **AutoPick Next** to propose a new meeting start and end time with the same time interval.
4. Click **Propose Time** to display the Meeting Response form.
5. In the **Message** text box, enter the response text.
6. Click **Send** to send the meeting request again with a new proposed time.

Procedure Reference: Accept a Suggested New Meeting Time

To accept a suggested new meeting time:

1. If necessary, open the Inbox.
2. Open the meeting request that you received with a proposed new meeting time.
3. On the **Meeting** tab, in the **Respond** group, click **Accept Proposal** to trigger an email to the person who proposed a new meeting time.
4. If necessary, close the original Meeting Request form.
5. If necessary, in the **Microsoft Office Outlook** message box, select the **Save Changes And Send Update** option, and click **OK.**

ACTIVITY 6-4
Responding to a Meeting Request

Scenario:
Your manager has invited you to discuss the accommodation and travel arrangements for participants to an upcoming seminar. Because you will not be available for the meeting discussing the accommodation, you want to keep him informed. You will however attend the other meeting.

1. Accept a meeting request.

    a. In the View pane, double-click the **Travel arrangement** meeting request and maximize the window.

    b. On the **Meeting** tab, in the **Respond** group, from the **Accept** drop-down list, select **Send the Response Now.**

    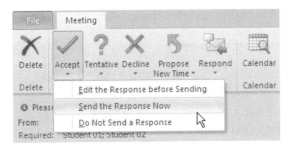

2. Send a reply to a meeting request and propose that it run from 2 to 2.30 P.M. instead.

    a. In the View pane, double-click the **Accommodation arrangements** meeting request.

    b. On the **Meeting** tab, in the **Respond** group, from the **Propose New Time** drop-down list, select **Decline and Propose New Time.**

    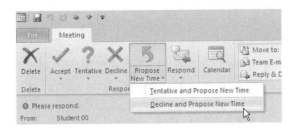

    c. In the **Propose New Time: Accommodation arrangements** dialog box, from the second **Meeting start** drop-down list, scroll up and select **2.30 PM.**

    d. Click **Propose Time.**

    e. In the message body, click and type *Can we meet at this time instead?* and click **Send.**

TOPIC C
Track and Update Scheduled Meetings

You replied to meeting requests. You may also need to track user responses, update a meeting, or cancel a meeting altogether. In this topic, you will track and update scheduled meetings.

For a meeting, you need to determine exactly how many people will be attending so that you can prepare the handouts. Depending on the response received, you might also need to update the meeting or cancel it and reschedule it for later. By using Outlook, you can quickly track who has responded and manage your meetings so that your schedule stays up-to-date.

How to Track and Update Scheduled Meetings

Procedure Reference: Track Meeting Responses

To track meeting responses:

1. Open a desired Meeting form.
2. On the **Meeting** tab, in the **Show** group, click **Tracking** to view the responses for the meeting.
3. If necessary, on the **Meeting** tab, click **Appointment** to view the Meeting form.

Procedure Reference: Update a Meeting Request

To update a meeting request:

1. Open the Meeting form that needs to be updated.
2. Make the appropriate changes to the **Meeting** form, such as changing the subject, entering the new start and end dates and times, and changing the location.
3. Send the update to the attendees.
   - In the **Meeting** form, click **Send Update** or;
   - In the **Meeting** form, click **Close** and, in the **Microsoft Office Outlook** message box, select the **Save Changes And Send Update** option, and click **OK**.

Procedure Reference: Send Meeting Updates Only to New Attendees

To send meeting updates only to new attendees:

1. Open the desired **Meeting** form.
2. In the **To** text box, delete the existing invitees.
3. On the **Meeting** tab, in the **Attendees** group, click **Add Or Remove Attendees.**
4. In the **Select Attendees and Resources: Global Address List,** select the desired invitee(s).
5. Click **Required** and then click **OK** to place the invitees' name(s) in the **To** text box.
6. In the Meeting form, click **Send Update.**
7. Select **Send Updates Only To Added Or Deleted Attendees** and click **OK**.

Procedure Reference: Modify an Instance of a Recurring Meeting

To modify one instance of a recurring meeting:

1. Open an instance of a recurring meeting.
2. Modify the meeting information as desired.

3. Click **Send Update.**
4. In the **Microsoft Outlook** message box, click **Yes.**
5. If necessary, close the original Meeting form.

Procedure Reference: Cancel a Meeting

To cancel a meeting:

1. In the calendar, select the meeting entry you want to cancel.
2. Cancel the meeting.
   - Open the Meeting form and, on the **Recurring Meeting** or **Meeting** tab, in the **Actions** group, click **Cancel Meeting** or;
   - Right-click the Meeting form and choose **Delete**, and in the **Confirm Delete** dialog box, delete the meeting or the series of meetings, and click **OK.** or;
   - On the Ribbon, in the **Delete** group, click **Delete,** and in the **Confirm Delete** dialog box, delete the meeting or the series of meetings, and click **OK.**
3. If desired, in the Meeting form, enter a message.
4. In the Meeting form, click **Send Cancellation** to send the cancellation message and remove the meeting from the calendar.

ACTIVITY 6-5
Updating a Meeting

Scenario:
One of your regular clients has requested you to reschedule an earlier appointment to the same time as the Vacation policy meeting. As there is a conflict of meeting times, you want to reschedule the Vacation policy meeting.

1. Update the Vacation policy meeting request.

   a. In the Quick Launch bar, click **Calendar.**

   b. In the Date Navigator section, select the upcoming Tuesday.

   c. In the Day view, double-click the **Vacation policy meeting.**

   d. In the message body, click and type *I am rescheduling it because I am meeting a client at this time.*

   e. In the Meeting form, in the second **Start Time** drop-down list, scroll down and select **1:00 PM.**

   f. Click **Send Update.**

2. Add an attendee to the meeting request.

   a. In the calendar, double click the **Vacation policy** meeting you scheduled.

   b. On the **Meeting** tab, in the **Attendees** group, click **Address Book.**

   c. In the **Select Attendees And Resources: Global Address List** dialog box, select your partner's user name.

   d. Click **Required** and then click **OK.**

3. Send the meeting update only to the new attendee.

   a. In the Meeting form, click **Send Update.**

b. In the **Send Updates to the Attendees** warning box, verify that the **Send updates only to added or deleted attendees** option is selected and click **OK**.

ACTIVITY 6-6
Rescheduling a Recurring Meeting

Scenario:

You have scheduled a recurring meeting for training new recruits. In one of the following weeks, you are invited to attend a mandatory meeting with senior management that conflicts with the time of the Training session. Therefore, you decide to change that particular occurrence of the training session and send the updated meeting request to the attendees. Further, as you are out of town the following week, you want to cancel the upcoming training session and send a cancellation message to all attendees.

1. Display the Meeting form.

    a. In the Date Navigator section, select the next Wednesday's date.

    b. In the Day view of the calendar, scroll down and double-click the **Training** meeting request.

    c. In the **Open Recurring Item** warning box, verify that the **Open this occurence** option is selected and click **OK** to open only this occurrence.

2. Modify the meeting details.

    a. In the Meeting form, from the first **Start time** drop-down list, select the upcoming Monday.

    b. Click **Send Update.**

    c. In the **Microsoft Outlook** warning box, click **Yes** to send the updated meeting request for this particular occurrence of the meeting.

3. Cancel a training session you scheduled and send a cancellation message to all attendees.

    a. In the Date Navigator section, select the Wednesday, which has the next training session scheduled.

    b. In the calendar, select the **Training** meeting that you scheduled.

c. On the **Meeting Series** contextual tab, in the **Actions** group, from the **Cancel Meeting** drop-down list, select **Cancel Occurrence**.

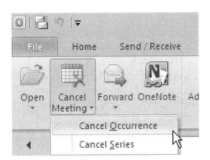

d. In the Meeting form, click **Send Cancellation**.

TOPIC D
Print the Calendar

You managed your meetings. Now you want to be able to check your appointments even when you are not logged in to your computer. In this topic, you will print the Outlook calendar.

You may have a number of appointments scheduled during the course of a trip, but you may not always have your computer along with you. By printing a copy of your calendar, you will know what your schedule is without needing your computer; and you do not have to worry about missing an appointment.

Print Styles

Outlook provides you with a range of styles for printing calendars. The styles are listed on the **Print** tab in the **Settings** section of the Backstage view.

Style	Prints
Daily Style	The current day's events with hourly time slots.
Weekly Agenda Style	The weekly events in the form of an agenda starting Monday through Sunday.
Weekly Calendar Style	The weekly events in the form of calendar entries in the respective dates.
Monthly Style	The events for the selected month.
Tri Fold Style	The events in the current day, the tasks list, and the weekly agenda.
Calendar Details Style	The details of all events scheduled in the calendar.

How to Print the Outlook Calendar

Procedure Reference: Print a Calendar

To print a calendar:
1. Ensure that the Outlook calendar is displayed.
2. On the Ribbon, select the **File** tab and choose **Print.**
3. In the Backstage view, in the **Settings** section, select a print style.
4. Above the **Print What** section, click **Print Options** to display the **Print** dialog box.
5. In the **Print** dialog box, specify the desired options and click **Print** to print the calendar.

ACTIVITY 6-7
Printing the Outlook Calendar

Scenario:
You have a meeting scheduled for the day after, and you learn that a few systems in your office have crashed and that data cannot be retrieved. You are cautious and want to take a printout of the scheduled appointments so that you do not miss any of them.

1. Display the Outlook calendar in the Work Week view.

   a. Observe that the Outlook calendar is displayed in the Day view.

   b. On the **Home** tab, in the **Arrange** group, click **Work Week** to view the calendar events from Monday through Friday.

   c. In the **Work Week** view, to the left of the month and year at the top of the pane, click the **Back** button to view the calendar for the next week.

2. Print the calendar.

   a. On the Ribbon, select the **File** tab and choose **Print.**

   b. In the Backstage view, in the **Printer** section, from the **Printer Status** drop-down list, select the desired printer.

   c. In the **Print What** section, observe that **Weekly Calendar Style** is selected.

   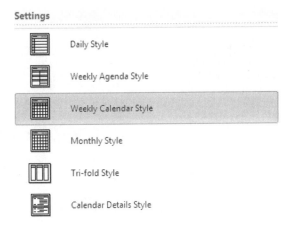

   d. In the **Print** section, click **Print** to print the calendar.

Lesson 6: Managing Meetings in Outlook

Lesson 6 Follow-up

In this lesson, you scheduled a meeting. Outlook lets you to organize meetings that involve any number of participants, and keep them informed about any changes that may occur in the schedule or location.

1. **What kinds of meetings have you proposed in your workplace? You may also elaborate on any conflicts relating to participant or resource availability faced by you.**

2. **What would be the reasons that compel you to tentatively agree to a meeting?**

7 Managing Tasks and Notes

Lesson Time: 45 minutes

Lesson Objectives:

In this lesson, you will manage tasks and notes.

You will:

- Create a task.
- Edit a task.
- Create a note.
- Edit a note.

Introduction

You scheduled appointments and meetings in Outlook. You can also keep track of the simple tasks that you perform and your ideas by using Outlook. In this lesson, you will manage tasks and notes.

While indulging in paperwork or pouring through pages of text, you jot down comments along the margin or scribble yourself a note. You may view these comments and notes as critical pieces of information that add value or shed perspective on the contents, but the chances of them getting lost in the pile are high. Outlook allows you to create notes, tasks, and reminders in such a way that it helps you to marshal your thoughts and actions in a few simple steps.

TOPIC A
Create a Task

You printed the meetings and appointments displayed in the Outlook calendar. Sometimes you may want to create a reminder about a project that doesn't need to go on your calendar, but you still need to track it progress. In this topic, you will create a task.

When you schedule an appointment or a meeting in Outlook, you are reminded about it at least 15 minutes before the scheduled time. Similarly, you can set a reminder for tasks in Outlook. This will also enable you to have an electronic list of what you need to do and when to do it.

Tasks

Definition:

A *task* is an assigned piece of work that must be completed within a certain time frame. It involves a single action or a set of actions that will result in a particular outcome.

Example:

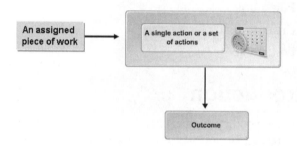

Figure 7-1: *A task that results in a particular outcome.*

Task Form

The *Task form* allows you to enter information pertaining to a task. It contains various controls that are used to enter details.

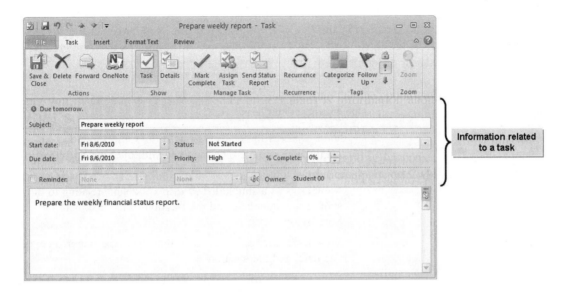

Figure 7-2: The Task form displaying the settings for a task with a reminder.

Text Box	Description
Subject	Displays the subject of the task.
Start date	Displays the date when the task should start.
Due date	Displays the date when the task should be completed.
Status	Displays one of five status choices: • **Not Started** • **In Progress** • **Completed** • **Waiting On Someone Else** • **Deferred**
Priority	Sets the priority to **Low, Normal,** or **High.**
% Complete	Displays the completion percentage of the task.
Reminder	Sets a reminder for the task along with a sound.
Owner	Displays the name of the person who set the task.
Note area	Displays any additional notes about the task.

Task Views

Tasks can be viewed in three places in the Outlook interface: in the View pane, in the **To-Do** bar, and in the **Daily Task** list in the calendar. Outlook also provides options to view created tasks and the list of tasks in different ways.

Task View	Enables You To
Detailed	View a task with details relating to its subject, the due date of completion, and the date modified with the **Sort by** options, and the location.
Simple List	View tasks as a simple list. It displays details relating to the subject, the due date, and the location of the task with the **Sort by** options.
To-Do List	View tasks arranged in order of their type, the importance, the due date, and the location.
Prioritized	View tasks in order of high, normal, and low priorities.
Active	View the ongoing tasks with details of the subject, percent complete, the status, due date and location.
Completed	View tasks that have been completed with details of the subject and the date on which they were completed.
Today	View tasks that have been scheduled for the day with details of the subject and due date.
Next 7 Days	View tasks that have been scheduled for the next seven days with details of the subject, percent complete, the status, and the due date.
Overdue	View tasks that are over due with details of the subject, percent complete, status, and due date.
Assigned	View tasks assigned to you with details of the owner, subject, status, and due date.

How to Create a Task

Procedure Reference: Create a Task

To create a task:

1. In the Navigation pane, click **Tasks** to display the **Tasks** list.
2. On the Home tab, in the **New** group, click **New Task** to display a new Task form.
3. In the Task form, in the **Subject** text box, enter a subject of your choice.
4. From the **Start Date** drop-down list, select a start date for the task.
5. From the **Due Date** drop-down list, select the date when the task is set for completion.
6. If necessary, from the **Priority** drop-down list, select a priority.
7. If necessary, set a reminder.
    a. Check the **Reminder** check box.
    b. From the **Reminder** drop-down lists, select a date and time when you want to be reminded of the task.
8. On the **Task** tab, in the **Actions** group, click **Save & Close**.

Procedure Reference: Create a Recurring Task

To create a recurring task:

1. Open a new Task form.
2. In the Task form, enter the task details such as the subject, start date, end date, and priority.
3. On the **Task** tab, in the **Options** group, click **Recurrence** to set the task as a recurring item.
4. In the **Task Recurrence** dialog box, in the **Recurrence Pattern** section, select the desired option.
5. In the **Range Of Recurrence** section, select the start and end date range and click **OK**.
6. Save and close the task.

Procedure Reference: Create a Task from a Message

To create a task from a message:

1. In the Inbox, select a message that has to be created as a task.
2. Set the follow-up date for a task.
    - On the **Home** tab, in the **Tags** group, from the **Follow Up** drop-down list, select the required flag option.
    - In the View pane, right-click a message and choose **Follow Up** and select the required flag option.
3. If necessary, verify that the flagged message is listed in the View pane.

Procedure Reference: Mark a Task Private

To mark a task private:

1. If necessary, in the View pane, double-click a task to open it, and on the **Task** tab, in the **Tags** group, click **Private**.
2. If necessary, in the View pane, select the desired task, and on the **Home** tab, in the **Tags** group, click **Private**.

3. Save and close the task.

Procedure Reference: Create a Meeting or an Appointment from a Task

To create an appointment from a task:
1. Display the task.
2. Add the task to the calendar.
   a. In the Task form, select the **File** tab.
   b. In the Backstage view, from the **Move to Folder** drop-down list, select **Other Folder.**
   c. In the **Move Item to** dialog box, select **Calendar** and click **OK.**
3. If necessary, check the **All Day Event** check box.
4. If necessary, create a meeting from the task.
   a. On the **Appointment** tab, in the **Attendees** group, click **Invite Attendees** to display the Meeting form.
   b. Add attendees and specify the resources for the meeting.
5. If necessary, change the date and time for the meeting or appointment.
6. Send the invite.

Procedure Reference: View Tasks Using Different Views

To view tasks using different views:
1. Display the Tasks list.
2. On the Ribbon, on the **View** tab, in the **Current View** group, click the **Change View** drop-down arrow to display the different views.
3. From the **Change View** drop-down list, select the desired view.

ACTIVITY 7-1
Creating a Task

Scenario:
You want to create a task for scheduling an appointment with your tax consultant. As this is an appointment that you want to be prepared for, you would like to be reminded about it a day before so that you can have adequate time to finalize the relevant documents.

1. Display a new Task form and enter the subject.

   a. In the Quick Launch bar, click **Tasks.**

   b. On the **Home** tab, in the **New** group, click **New Task** to display a new Task form.

   c. Maximize the Task form.

   d. In the **Subject** text box, type *Tax consultation*

2. Set the date for the task to two weeks from today.

   a. Click the **Due Date** drop-down arrow.

   b. In the calendar that is displayed, select the date two weeks from today.

3. Set the priority and reminder for the task and set it as a private task.

   a. In the Task form, from the **Priority** drop-down list, select **High.**

   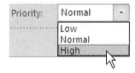

   b. Check the **Reminder** check box.

   c. Click the **Reminder** drop-down arrow, and in the calendar that is displayed, select a date before the due date.

   d. On the **Task** tab, in the **Tags** group, click **Private.**

   e. On the **Task** tab, in the **Actions** group, click **Save & Close.**

Microsoft® Office Outlook® 2010: Level 1

ACTIVITY 7-2
Creating Recurring Tasks

Scenario:
You want to prepare a status report to keep your team updated on work related developments. As you plan to do this regularly, you want to schedule this as a recurring task.

1. Display a new Task form and enter the subject.

    a. On the **Home** tab, in the **New** group, click **New Task.**

    b. In the **Task** form, in the **Subject** text box, type *Prepare weekly report*

    c. Click the **Start Date** drop-down arrow, and in the calendar displayed, select the forth coming Friday.

    d. Click the **Due date** drop-down arrow, and in the calendar that is displayed, navigate through six months from the current month.

    e. Select the last Friday of that month. The selected date is displayed in the **Due Date** text box.

    f. In the Task form, from the **Priority** drop-down list, select **High.**

2. Set the Prepare weekly report task as a recurring task.

    a. On the **Task** tab, in the **Recurrence** group, click **Recurrence** to set the task as a recurring item.

    b. In the **Task recurrence** dialog box, in the **Recurrence pattern** section, verify that the **Weekly** option is selected.

    c. In the **Range of recurrence** section, click the **End by** drop-down arrow.

    d. In the calendar that is displayed, navigate to and display the month that is six months from the start date.

    e. Select the date six months from the start date and click **OK** to return to the Prepare weekly report- Task form.

    f. In the **Actions** group, click **Save & Close.**

178   Lesson 7: Managing Tasks and Notes

TOPIC B
Edit and Update a Task

You created a task. At some point in time, you may want to make changes to the task you created. In this topic, you will edit and update tasks.

You do not have to delete a task to create a new one with a revised date. Instead, you can simply edit the task, ensuring that the task information is accurate and up-to-date.

How to Edit and Update a Task

Procedure Reference: Edit a Task

To edit a task:

1. If necessary, display the **Tasks** list.
2. Open the task you want to edit.
3. Make the appropriate changes in the Task form.
4. Save the task and close the Task form.

Procedure Reference: Update a Task

To update a task:

1. If necessary, display the Tasks list.
2. Select the desired task.
3. Mark a task as complete.
    - On the **Home** tab, in the **Manage Task** group, click **Mark Complete** to mark the task you have completed.
    - In the **Flag Status** column, click the flag of the task you have completed.
    - In the **Complete** column of the selected task, check the check box.

ACTIVITY 7-3
Editing and Updating a Task

Scenario:
You have a recurring task: preparing weekly reports for your colleagues. Because it is more effective to provide information in a presentation format, you decide to document this change. You also want to set a reminder for this task so that you will have advance notice to prepare for the presentation. Meanwhile, on another task, your tax consultant has confirmed receiving the documents you sent; he feels that there is no need for a meeting now. You want to mark this task as completed.

1. Edit the Prepare weekly report task.

    a. In the To-Do list view, double-click the **Prepare weekly report** task.

    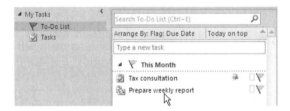

     You can also select the item you want to edit and press **Enter** to open it.

    b. In the **Subject** text box, double-click the word **"report"** to select it.

    c. Type *presentation*

2. Set a reminder for the recurring task.

    a. In the Task form, check the **Reminder** check box.

    b. In the second **Reminder** drop-down list, scroll down and select **4:00 PM**.

    c. Click **Save & Close**.

3. Mark the **Tax consultation** task as complete.

    a. On the **View** tab, in the **Current View** group, from the **Change View** drop-down list, select **Simple List** to display the tasks as a simple list with different column names.

b. To the left of the **Tax consultation** task, check the check box to mark the task as complete.

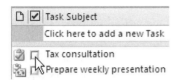

c. Observe that the **Tax consultation** task is crossed off, and on the Quick Launch bar, click **Mail** to return to the Outlook window.

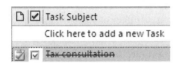

TOPIC C
Create a Note

You created tasks in Outlook and used them to track the progress of assignments. You may also want to jot down ideas or thoughts while working on your system. In this topic, you will create a note.

While composing a message, you remember an issue that you wanted to bring up in the department meeting. With Outlook, you can quickly document your thoughts and ideas for easy reference later.

Notes

Outlook *Notes* is a feature that enables you to capture bits of information that you don't want to lose or forget. A note can be created and assigned a color category for easy identification. Notes can be sorted by date, category, or subject.

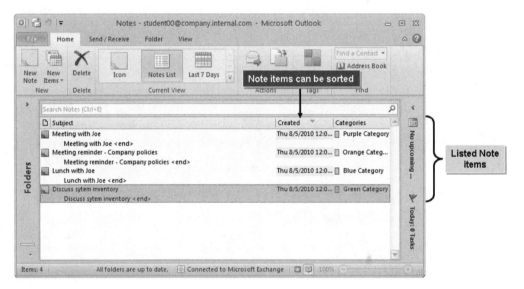

Figure 7-3: Information captured as notes.

How to Create a Note

Procedure Reference: Create a Note

To create a note:

1. In the Navigation pane, click **Notes** to display the Notes folder.
2. Create a new note.
   - On the **Home** tab, in the **New** group, click **New Note.**
   - On the **Home** tab, in the **New** group, click the drop-down arrow next to **New Items** and choose **More Items→Note.**
3. Type the content of the note.
4. If necessary, assign a color category to the note.
5. If necessary, place the mouse pointer on the resizing handle until a double-headed arrow is displayed and drag to resize the note.
6. Click **Close** to close the note.

Options for Viewing Notes

You can choose the view you want for your notes by selecting an option on the **Home** tab in the **Current View** group.

- **Icons**: View notes as icons.
- **Notes List**: View notes as a list.
- **Last Seven Days**: View notes that you worked with in the last seven days.
- **By Category**: View notes based on the color categories.
- **Outlook Data Files**: View notes based on the names of the data files attached to the notes.

ACTIVITY 7-4
Creating a Note

Scenario:
While managing your Outlook tasks, you remember that the company policy regarding personal email has to be communicated to the employees. You will add it to a meeting agenda later, but for now you just want to jot it down somewhere so that you don't forget it.

1. In the Notes folder, display a new note.

   a. On the Quick Launch bar, click **Notes**.

   b. On the **Home** tab, in the **New** group, click **New Note**.

2. Write a note on the meeting reminder and assign it to the **Business** category.

   a. Type *Meeting Reminder: Company policy regarding personal email.*

   b. In the top left corner of the note, click the **Note** icon.

   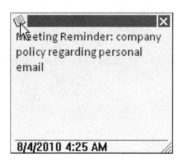

   c. Choose **Categorize→Business**.

3. Decrease the size of the note and close it.

a. Click the lower-right corner of the note and drag up and to the left by an inch to resize the note.

b. Click the **Close** button.

TOPIC D
Edit a Note

You have created a note. You might need to update the information that a note displays. In this topic, you will edit the contents of a note.

Perhaps you have more thoughts and ideas about something that you do not want to forget, and want to add it to an existing note. You can easily edit an existing note, ensuring that your thoughts and ideas are accurately documented in the right place.

How to Edit a Note

Procedure Reference: Edit a Note

To edit a Note:

1. If necessary, display the Notes folder.
2. Open the note you want to edit.
    - Select the note and press **Enter,** or;
    - Double-click the note, or;
    - Right-click the note and choose **Open.**
3. Edit the content of the note as desired.
4. If necessary, change the color category of the note.
5. If necessary, resize the note.
6. Close the note.

Procedure Reference: Copy a Note to the Desktop

To copy a Note to the desktop:

1. If necessary, display the Notes folder.
2. Adjust the size of the Outlook window so that the desktop is visible.
3. Drag the note you want to copy to the desktop.

 You can also copy or move a note to other folders.

ACTIVITY 7-5
Editing a Note

Scenario:
You just remembered that in addition to clarifying the company's policy on personal email, you want to make sure you distribute a copy of the company policy to employees. You decide to change the color category of your note, so that you can locate it easily. You also want to display the note on your desktop so that you can access it even without launching the application.

1. Edit the content of the note.

   a. In the Notes folder, verify that the **Meeting Reminder: Company policy regarding personal email** note is selected and press **Enter** to open it.

   b. Place the insertion point before the word "Company."

   c. Type *Present and distribute* and press the **Spacebar.**

   d. Resize the note to view its entire content.

2. Change the color category of the note to "Red."

   a. In the top left corner of the note, click the **Note** icon and choose **Categorize→ Business** to remove the assignment of **Business** category to the note.

   b. Assign the **Red** Category to the note.

   c. In the **Rename Category** dialog box, in the **Name** text box, type *Important* and click **Yes.**

   d. Close the note.

3. Display a portion of the desktop and copy the note to it.

   a. To the left of the **Close** button, click the **Restore Down** button.

   b. If necessary, position the mouse pointer over any corner of the window and adjust the size of the window so that the content of the Notes folder and the desktop are visible.

   c. Drag the note from the Notes folder to the desktop.

   d. Observe that a copy of the note is displayed on the desktop, and close the Outlook application.

   e. In the **Microsoft Outlook** message box, click **Yes.**

Lesson 7 Follow-up

In this lesson, you created and edited tasks and notes. Now when you have tasks or want to jot down notes, you will be able to do so, secure in the knowledge that you can manage daily tasks and not lose valuable bits of information.

1. **When working on a project, what kind of information do you have to keep track of so that it could be stored in the tasks list?**

2. **What do you frequently jot down on sticky notes? Would using Outlook Notes for the same be helpful?**

Follow-up

In this course, you mastered the essential skills required for using Outlook to meet your communication needs.

1. Which form in Outlook would you use the most frequently? Why?

2. Of the tools covered in this course, which one will you use the most? Which one will you use the least?

3. What do you feel is the biggest advantage of using Outlook 2010? Why?

What's Next?

Microsoft® Office Outlook® 2010: Level 2 is the next course in the series. In this course, you will customize the Outlook environment, calendar, and mail messages to meet your specific needs. You will also track, share, assign, and quickly locate various items in Outlook.

Lesson Labs

Lesson labs are provided as an additional learning resource for this course. The labs may or may not be performed as part of the classroom activities. Your instructor will consider setup issues, classroom timing issues, and instructional needs to determine which labs are appropriate for you to perform, and at what point during the class. If you do not perform the labs in class, your instructor can tell you if you can perform them independently as self-study, and if there are any special setup requirements.

Lesson 1 Lab 1
Exploring the Outlook Environment

Activity Time: 10 minutes

Before You Begin:
Send a few messages to your email account from another account.

Scenario:
Your company has purchased and installed Outlook 2010 with the expectation that all employees will use it for electronic messaging. You are anxious to start using Outlook, but before doing so, you need to explore the Outlook environment and identify some Outlook tools, in order to begin building a foundation for moving forward and using the application. You also notice that a few messages are already displayed in your Inbox. You decide to read some of these messages. You also want to reply to a message and delete some messages from your Inbox.

1. Launch Outlook.

2. Select the **File** tab to view the options in the Backstage view.

3. Explore the commands on the **Home** tab.

4. Preview a message that you have received in your Inbox.

5. Open and reply to a message.

6. If necessary, close the original message.

7. Delete unwanted messages from the Inbox.

8. Set the option to delete the messages permanently from the Deleted Items folder.

Microsoft® Office Outlook® 2010: Level 1

Lesson 2 Lab 1
Composing Messages Using Outlook

Activity Time: 10 minutes

Data Files:

C:\084595Data\Composing Messages\SS Resume.docx

Scenario:

You have a friend who is interested in working at Our Global Company. She has given you her resume to pass it on to your manager.

1. Create a message and address it to your partner by using the **Global Address List.**

    If a partner is not available, then you can act the role and send the message to yourself.

2. Add an appropriate subject for the message.

3. Apply the formatting of your choice to the message text.

4. From the C:\084595Data\Composing Messages folder, attach the SS Resume.docx file to the message.

5. Check the message for spelling and grammatical errors.

6. Send the message to your contact.

Lesson Labs

Lesson 3 Lab 1
Managing Email Messages

Activity Time: 10 minutes

Before You Begin:
1. Compose and send messages to a few contacts.
2. Send a few messages to your Inbox from another email account.

Scenario:

As a senior executive in your company, you know that staying organized is key to your success. You have a number of messages in your Inbox related to an upcoming recruitment program. It will be easy to refer to those messages if they are together in one location, and flagged appropriately.

1. Create a subfolder called *Business* in the Inbox.

2. Move a message of your choice into the new folder.

3. Create two folders named *Clients* and *Candidates.*

4. Move the Clients and Candidates folders to the Business folder.

5. Flag important messages.

6. Delete unwanted folders, if any.

Lesson 4 Lab 1
Creating Contacts

Activity Time: 10 minutes

Scenario:

You met a placement specialist at a recent training conference you attended. You do not want to lose his contact information, which is listed below.

- Name: Roger Gorman
- Business address: 23 Colonial Way, Syracuse, NY 14388
- Business phone: 315–555–9090
- Email address: rogergorman@ourglobalcompany.example
- Home address: 33 Sylvia Way, Baldwinsville, NY 14378

After reviewing your contacts in various views, you remember to include "Rog" as a nickname for the newly added contact.

1. Add the contact to the Outlook address book by using the details given in the scenario.

2. Save and close the Contact form.

3. Similarly, add a few more contacts with the details of your choice.

4. Practice viewing your contacts by using different views.

5. Include *Rog* as a nickname for the newly added contact.

Lesson 5 Lab 1
Using the Calendar

Activity Time: 10 minutes

Scenario:

You are coaching your company's soccer team this season. The practices are at Hyde Park, from 4:30 PM to 7:30 PM, every Thursday through the next two months. Also, you are asked to meet for a private lunch with your manager at The Garden, this upcoming Monday from 2:00 PM to 2:30 PM.

1. Create a new recurring appointment for the soccer practices at Hyde Park, from 4:30 PM to 7:30 PM, each Thursday for the next two months.

2. Check your calendar to verify that the recurring appointment is scheduled.

3. Create an appointment for a working lunch with your manager.

4. Mark this appointment private and assign a category of **Personal.**

Lesson 6 Lab 1
Scheduling Meetings

Activity Time: 10 minutes

Scenario:

For a meeting with a colleague to discuss next year's budget requirements, you check his calendar for availability and decide to schedule it for the coming Thursday at 2:30 PM. You send a meeting request to your colleague, marking it private. He accepts the meeting request. On the other hand, your manager has sent you a schedule that will require you to do some amount of travelling on the same day. It is high priority work and, therefore, you cancel the meeting by sending a notice explaining your reasons.

1. Schedule a one-hour **Budget** meeting with your partner for the upcoming Thursday.

    If a partner is not available, then you can playact the role and send the message to yourself.

2. Mark this meeting **Private.**

3. Accept the meeting request, including a message of your choice.

4. Cancel the **Budget** meeting you scheduled, and send a cancellation notice explaining the reasons.

Lesson 7 Lab 1
Creating Tasks and Notes

Activity Time: 10 minutes

Scenario:

You are in charge of an upcoming job fair at a local community college. Among the many tasks you must complete is a discussion with a representative of a college to finalize your space requirements. You also want to create a separate task to keep track of how the arrangements are progressing. Because of the confidential nature of these discussions, you want to flag this task as private. While you are doing this work, you need to jot down a couple of notes so that you can refer to them later in the week.

1. Create a task for the meeting with the subject as **Space Requirements** and an appropriate start and due date.

2. Create a recurring task for discussing the progress of the job fair arrangements with the subject of **Job fair progress** and set it as a recurring task for the next four Wednesdays.

3. Mark the Job Fair Requirements task as **Private.**

4. In the Notes folder, create two notes with the content of your choice and assign an appropriate category to each.

Solutions

Activity 2-4

2. **Which information will be displayed for an attached file?**

    ✓ a) File name

    ✓ b) File type

    ✓ c) File size

       d) File creation date

Glossary

Appointment form
A form that contains options for entering specific information to create an appointment.

Attachment Preview
A feature that allows you to preview a file that is attached to an email message.

attachment
A copy of any type of file or item that needs to be included along with an email.

AutoCorrect
A feature that detects common typing mistakes, including misspelled words, grammar, incorrect capitalization, and common typos.

AutoPreview
A feature in Outlook that enables you to preview the first few lines of a message without actually opening it.

Backstage view
A File menu view with a series of tabs that group similar commands and provides options for managing stored Outlook application data.

color category
An Outlook feature that allows you to assign color codes to related Outlook items.

Contact form
A form that contains tabs and text boxes in which you can enter personal and business information.

contact views
A feature that helps you find and view information in your preferred style.

contact
A person with whom you communicate on a business or personal level.

Conversation
A view that enables you to view groups of messages that share the same subject.

dialog box launchers
The small downward-pointing arrow buttons that help launch the relevant dialog box with advanced setting options.

electronic business card
A feature that is used to share information about a contact through email.

email address
A string used to specify the user name and domain where users can send email messages.

email
A message that is sent electronically using a standard email application.

flag
A feature that has an icon to indicate whether the message needs follow up attention.

forward
A message that is sent to another person who has not already received it.

gallery
A library that lists a set of predefined styles that can be used when composing a message.

Global Address List
A list of the email addresses of different contacts in an organization that is created and maintained by the Microsoft Exchange Server administrator.

InfoBar
A bar that displays information about what has occurred or what action you need to take in the mail box.

Live Preview
A feature that enables users to preview the result of applying design and formatting changes to a message in real time, without actually applying them.

MailTips
A feature that provides real-time feedback on messages before sending them.

Map It
An option that helps you locate the address of a contact in a visual format.

Meeting form
A form that contains options to schedule a meeting.

meeting resource
A facility or equipment that is used during a meeting.

Microsoft Exchange Server
A mail server that manages email messages on a network.

Mini toolbar
A floating toolbar that appears beside the selected text, and consists of commonly used font and paragraph tools.

Notes
A feature that allows you to capture miscellaneous bits of information that you don't want to lose or forget.

personal folders
The mail folders that are located on the local hard drive.

Ribbon
A tabular component at the top of the user interface that provides quick access to task-specific commands.

Room Finder pane
A pane in the Meeting form that helps you to locate a room for a meeting.

ScreenTips
A small window that displays descriptive text upon pointing the mouse over a command, button, or a control.

SmartArt
A visual representation of ideas that can be added to Outlook mail messages to enhance the presentation of information.

sort order
The sequence in which items are arranged.

Style
A collection of format options applied to modify the appearance of draft messages .

Task form
A form that contains controls where you can enter information pertaining to a task.

task
A set of actions that must be completed in a defined period of time.

The Address Book
A collection of address lists that stores contact information.

Theme
A custom design that is applied to an application.

translation
A feature that translates selected text into a different language.

wildcard
A special symbol that can represent one or more characters.

Index

A
address books, 36
  secondary, 101
Appointment forms, 132
  components of, 132
  launching, 133
appointment reminders, 134
attachments, 53
  deleting, 92
  guidelines to the file type & size, 54
  opening, 92
  previewing, 91
  saving, 92

B
Backstage view, 5

C
calendar
  previewing, 159
Calendar Attendant, 149
color categories, 100
commands
  Clean Up, 77
  Ignore, 77
Contact forms, 98
  options for, 99
contact views, 100
contacts, 98
  adding, 101
  adding a picture to, 118
  assigning categories to, 102
  creating from one another, 102
  displaying, 102
  editing details of, 118
  finding, 113
Contacts list
  creating a message, 39
conversations, 16

D
default email folders, 84
dialog box launchers, 5
dialog boxes
  AutoCorrect, 46
  Print, 27
  Spelling and Grammar, 46

E
electronic business cards, 100
email, 15
email addresses, 36

F
features in Outlook
  Auto Empty, 30
  AutoCorrect, 46
  AutoPreview, 16
  Live Preview, 41
  translation, 47
folders
  moving, 86

G
galleries, 58
Global Address lists, 37
  creating a message, 39
groups
  Find, 112

I

Inbox, 6
InfoBar, 24

M

maps, 116
  generating, 116
meeting
  conflicts, 159
  marking as private, 151
  recurring, 151
  resources, 148
  responding to a request, 159
  scheduling, 146
  suggesting a new time, 160
  tracking responses, 162
Meeting form, 147
message flags, 76
Message forms, 37
  composing a message, 39
messages
  addressing, 70
  applying themes to, 61
  attaching files to, 54
  checking the spelling & grammar of, 48
  deleting, 31
  formatting, 42
  forwarding, 24
  marking as unread, 79
  moving to folders, 85
  opening, 18
  previewing, 18
  printing, 28
  resending, 70
  saving, 70
  sending, 70
  setting a default font for, 61
  using symbols, 17
Microsoft Exchange Server, 37
Microsoft Office Outlook 2010, 2
Microsoft Office Outlook 2010 window
  components of, 2

O

options
  for private appointments, 140
  mail tracking, 24
Map It, 116

replying to messages, 23
Set Quick Click, 79
Outlook calendar, 128
  displaying, 130
  symbols for, 133
  types of entries in, 129
  views of, 129
Outlook folders, 6
Outlook Help
  options in, 8
Outlook items, 6

P

panes
  Reading, 18
  View, 6
personal folders, 84
  creating, 85
print styles, 168

R

Ribbon, 3
Room Finder pane, 148

S

Scheduling Assistant, 148
ScreenTips, 4
searchable terms, 114
SmartArt, 59
sort order, 112
styles, 59

T

tabs
  contextual, 56
  Tool, 57
Task form, 172
tasks, 172
  marking as private, 175
  recurring, 175
  updating, 179
  views, 174
text
  formatting using the Mini toolbar, 43
themes, 59
toolbars
  Mini, 41
  Outlook Help, 8

tools
 Background Removal, 61
 Screenshot, 60

W

wildcards, 9